Ferns

TIME
LIFE
BOOKS
®

Other Publications:

Ferns

by
PHILIP PERL
and
the Editors of TIME-LIFE BOOKS

Watercolor Illustrations by
Richard Crist

TIME-LIFE BOOKS, ALEXANDRIA, VIRGINIA

THE AUTHOR: Philip Perl was born in Manhattan and educated at Columbia University. He was on the staff of *The New Yorker* magazine for 20 years. In addition to writing about plants, he works with them as a garden designer and interior landscaper. He is also a partner in a retail plant shop in New York City.

THE ILLUSTRATOR: Richard Crist provided the watercolor paintings for this book. He studied at Carnegie Institute of Technology and The Art Institute of Chicago. An amateur botanist, Mr. Crist is the author of several children's books.

GENERAL CONSULTANTS: Author of 13 of the volumes in the Encyclopedia, co-author of two additional volumes, and consultant on other books in the series, James Underwood Crockett has been a lover of the earth and its good things since his boyhood on a Massachusetts fruit farm. He was graduated from the Stockbridge School of Agriculture at the University of Massachusetts and has worked ever since in horticulture. A perennial contributor to leading gardening magazines, he also writes a monthly bulletin, "Flowery Talks," that is widely distributed through retail florists. His television program, *Crockett's Victory Garden,* shown all over the United States, is constantly winning new converts to the Crockett approach to growing things. Dr. Bruce W. McAlpin is Horticultural Specialist for the tropical plant and fern collections at the New York Botanical Garden. Barbara Joe Hoshizaki is Professor of Botany at Los Angeles City College, Curator of Ferns at the University of California at Los Angeles, and author of *Fern Growers Manual.* Dr. John Mickel is Curator of Ferns at the New York Botanical Garden.

THE COVER: Massed in harmonious color, form and texture is a sampler of the almost infinite variety of ferns that can be grown at home, some indoors, some outdoors. In the center is a squirrel's-foot fern and surrounding it, clockwise from the top, a button fern, a pink-tinged maidenhair named Martha's Pride, a fluffy variety of Boston fern, an Australian cliff brake, a silver brake fern, a rosy maidenhair, a holly fern and a maidenhair named Gracillimum.

Portions of this book were written by Marilyn Bethany, Mary V. O'Gorman, Jane Opper and
Barbara Ann Peters.

CONTENTS

Beauty without bloom 1

The fern is at once the most popular and the most neglected of plants. It is often the first house plant children are introduced to, since a fern in the parlor is an American tradition. It is usually the Boston fern, named for the city where it was first marketed in 1894. During the 1970s, two million Boston ferns a year were being sold in the United States, about one to every 25 families.

Those who did not encounter their first ferns in the parlor might have done so on a foray into the woods. The meeting is memorable to many—that first spring sighting of the cinnamon fern, its crosiers just beginning to uncoil from their cinnamon-colored woolly casings, or the surprise of the autumnal smell of new-mown forage drifting from a dense growth of hay-scented ferns. The unexpected and tranquil beauty of wild ferns impresses everyone who happens upon them for the first time.

Still, until recently it has been the rare gardener who attempted to grow ferns without previously having tried everything else. This neglect is understandable: the fern is hardly the kind of spectacular plant likely to bedazzle visitors; since it lacks both flowers and fruit, its delicate beauty is easily missed. Moreover, its culture is different from that demanded by other plants, although it is not particularly more difficult. It requires carefully metered moisture, high humidity, sometimes specialized nutrients and measured illumination. And its propagation processes are so unusual that they mystified scientists until the mid-19th Century. Yet once ferns have been given their proper place in the sun—or in the shade—they will delight the gardener with their modest demands on both time and pocketbook.

Today the neglect of ferns is coming to an end. They are the interior designers' favorite, crowding costly restaurants and fashionable apartments. Plain dirt gardeners, too, are responding to the challenges of growing ferns outdoors in the garden as well as

In a typically opulent "Wardian case," tropical ferns, a bromeliad and a vining cissus (center) flourish. This 6-foot Victorian terrarium was modeled after the Crystal Palace of London's Great Exhibition of 1851.

indoors in pots. The ranks of fern enthusiasts have swelled. The Los Angeles International Fern Society, for example, which was founded in 1959 with only 50 members, had topped the 5,000 mark in membership less than 20 years later. A Florida fern retailer reported at about the same time that his sales had doubled in a five-year period. When the New York Botanical Garden, with the American Fern Society, staged its first fern festival in 1977, more than 10,000 fern fanciers turned up.

INTEREST RENEWED

The boom in ferns is not so much a new phenomenon as a resurgence of interest that had waned for many decades after reaching the proportions of a mania in Britain in the 19th Century. At that time the passion for ferns was so intense that one grower offered more than 50 varieties of the hart's-tongue fern alone—

THE SHAPES OF FRONDS

1. *At its simplest a fern leaf, or frond, has a center vein that bisects a leafy blade. This type of frond, described as uncut because it lacks the divisions in the blade common to most ferns, gives species such as the hart's-tongue fern an atypical sturdiness.*

2. *The fronds of ferns like the Boston fern are described as once-cut because each side of the blade is divided into leaflets. The divisions extend to the central vein, whose branches bisect each leaflet.*

3. *A twice-cut fern is so called because the blade is divided into leaflets which, in turn, are divided into subleaflets. The lady fern is typical; each leafy branch is a microcosm of a simpler frond.*

4. *The progression continues—and ends—with a thrice-cut frond, the type found in davallias. Although growers have succeeded in cultivating fronds cut four and even five times, these varieties, left unattended, automatically revert to a more stable, thrice-cut pattern.*

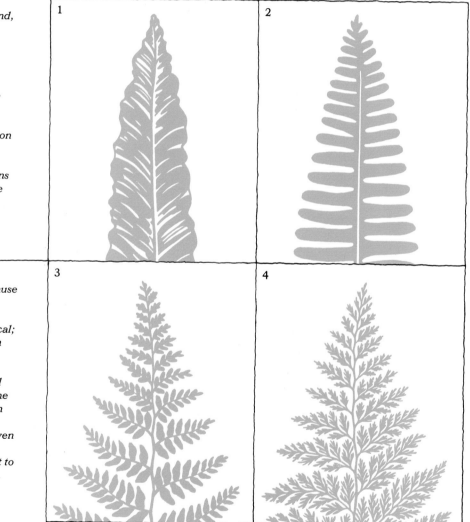

charging for some varieties as much as two guineas each, an enormous sum of money to spend for a plant in those days, equivalent to about $50 a century later.

Indigenous ferns were available in England, but the first exotic ferns—two species—came from Madeira in 1699, and 37 more species were brought from the West Indies in 1795 by Captain William Bligh, whose legendary despotism had triggered the mutiny on the *Bounty* six years earlier. Admired though the ferns were by those who saw them, they remained unattainable curiosities for most people because of the high cost of transporting them from the tropics and the huge losses that occurred on the voyages.

ARTIFICIAL PROPAGATION

Captain Bligh did not know it at the time, but he was to be spared the trouble of bringing up more ferns from the West Indies. Before his plants had even been loaded aboard ship in the Antilles, a physician named John Lindsay, who lived in Jamaica, notified a London botanical society that he had found a way to propagate ferns, even though neither he nor anyone else understood the process at that time. Word of Lindsay's method spread quickly. British greenhouses were soon able to offer vast numbers of tropical ferns. All that was missing were the customers.

The catalyst who set off the fern boom was Nathaniel Ward, a physician by profession but a botanist by preference. He was obliged to confine his botanical pursuits to his backyard, where he had built a fern rockery. To his consternation, the ferns kept dying, victims of the noxious fumes that were spewed into his garden by the city's factories.

While trying to keep his ferns alive, Ward also had been studying moths, and he had placed a cocoon in a covered jar, hoping to see the emerging larva. Probably distracted by the twin emergencies of sick ferns and sick patients (the same fumes that were poisoning his ferns were plaguing his customers), he apparently forgot his captive moth. Six months later, he noticed that, though the cocoon was still dormant, several plants had grown in the bit of soil at the bottom of the jar, among them a male fern. Unlike the ferns in his garden, it looked healthy. The conclusion was inescapable: plants could flourish in the London of the 1830s if they could be protected from the city's foul air. Ward pursued his discovery in miniature greenhouses, which he named fern cases but which are now known, in honor of their inventor, as Wardian cases.

A DOMESTIC NECESSITY

The fern case was just what pollution-oppressed Londoners, seeking a durable bit of greenery to brighten their lives, wanted, and it became, in various guises, almost a domestic necessity. The poor had to content themselves with inexpensive rudimentary versions, but there were no limits for the rich. Wardian cases grew into miniature Taj Mahals and Brighton Pavilions *(page 6),* perfect vehicles for the contemporary love of elaborate ornamentation as well as living plants. Ferns eventually had to share their cases with an expanding assortment of what would now be called terrarium plants, and ultimately with reptiles and other small animals in a construction known today as a vivarium.

English greenhousemen outdid themselves in introducing new tropical varieties to fill the fern cases. Fern fanciers who could not afford the prices took to the countryside in such numbers that local woods were denuded of native ferns and it became necessary to travel farther and farther to get at them. The first cries for conservation began to be heard. "We must have fern laws and preserve them like game," cried a Victorian lady named Nona Bellairs, perhaps in contrition over her own part in the plunder, for she went on to add: "I did what I advise other fern lovers to do: I packed up a large hamper full, and sent it off by rail, home." Those fern fanciers unable to pick their own often relied on "fern robbers," indigent youths who brought ferns from the country and hawked them in the streets of London.

At the height of the mania, ferns were cherished even in their harvest, for there was a thriving trade in pressed ferns, neatly framed and labeled, and highly suitable for hanging on busy Victorian walls. There were even ferns underfoot, for the rugs in the parlor were covered with patterns of intertwined fronds in many shades of green, always on black backgrounds. Though the Victorians did not eat ferns, as the Hawaiians did, they apparently could not eat without them; silver ferns ornamented the flatware of the day, and baskets of real ferns graced the dining tables; some of these baskets had holes cut in their sides so that large ferns could protrude and be admired during dinner. About the only places where ferns were not to be found were the fields and forests, largely stripped clean to indulge the mania. There is no record of the craze crossing either the Atlantic Ocean or the English Channel. The Wardian case itself apparently was fashionable in the United States in the early 1860s, but it did not precipitate a fern craze as it had in Great Britain. Undoubtedly Americans were too busy fighting the Civil War to pay much attention to ferns.

The British fern mania was made possible by John Lindsay's 1794 discovery of a practical propagation method, but it was stimulated by the later discovery of the curious sex life of these plants. The fecundity of ferns is unquestionable; they evolved some 350 million years ago and became spectacularly abundant during the

Carboniferous period, often called the Age of Ferns. Most ancient ferns have disappeared, although there are some that have not changed. Most people would probably recognize the royal fern (*Osmunda regalis*), thoroughly at home in a bog, with its fertile spikes looking, except for their dark green color, like spikes of heather or lavender. Another ancient fern, the *Lyginopteris,* would be totally unfamiliar. A climbing fern now extinct, it not only bore seeds but covered itself with a new band of wood every year, which made its growth distinctly unfernlike. Towering above would be the tree ferns, which survive in tropical regions in smaller form. They would appear wildly incongruous, like generously spreading ferns that have been uprooted from a comfortable garden and placed upon pikestaffs 100 feet high. (Other gargantuan prehistoric plants might include 60-foot horsetails, looking, except for their height, just as they do today, and club mosses 50 feet high.)

The greatest legacy of the Age of Ferns is coal, some seven trillion tons of it worldwide. Over the millennia fern and other plant debris piled up in the swamps and bogs and was transformed by decomposition and pressure into peat, then into coal. Within the coal formations survive perfect fossils, from which much knowledge of prehistoric ferns is derived.

One of the first serious students of ferns was Pedanius Dioscorides, a Greek physician who served with Nero's Roman armies. He made use of one variety of fern to treat ailments of the spleen, then thought to be a seat of emotions. The fern thus used became known as the spleenwort, a name that has stuck to this day. (There are at least 10 hardy spleenworts, all of them beautiful and worth growing even if there is nothing wrong with your spleen.)

Pliny the Elder, a Roman naturalist who was a contemporary of Dioscorides, is credited with first recording the fact that ferns bear neither flowers nor seeds, an observation that was to intrigue fern watchers and subject the fern to centuries of superstition. A thousand years after Pliny, botanists still were at a loss to explain how the flowerless, seedless fern could reproduce, and they outdid one another in the invention of imaginary fern seeds, flowers and mystical power. In 1592, William Turner, the father of English botany, described in his *Herbal* the gathering of fern seed, which he likened in appearance to that of the poppy. The seed appeared only on Midsummer Eve (June 21), he wrote, and was coveted because it supposedly would make the bearer invisible. Potential seed gatherers had to be prepared to fight off Oberon, the king of the fairies, who derived his invisibility from it and understandably did not want to share the secret with anyone else.

The great age of ferns—which evolved long before there were any flowering plants—is indicated by this 9-inch fragment of a fossil fern, Pecopteris miltoni artis, found in an Illinois coal mine. Although it lived 280 million years ago in a Paleozoic-era swamp, it looks almost exactly like a modern fern.

Legends about ferns persisted until the 18th Century, growing more bizarre with the passage of time. A good example is the story of a certain South China tree fern, which has a covering of fleecy golden hairs at the base of its leafstalks. Medieval botanists decided the fleece came from a lamb that grew on a stalk and had a root connecting its navel with the ground. The animal could turn about on the stalk and nibble on the vegetation around it. When it ran out of food, it died, since it was unable to move to a new feeding ground. The myth itself died in 1725, when a curious student subjected the fern lamb to its first scientific analysis and found it to be only a tree-fern stem swathed in fleecy hair.

REPRODUCTION UNRAVELED

The other legends about ferns were similarly eradicated as serious scientific study during the 19th Century finally unraveled the puzzle of the reproductive system of the plants. It was not until 1851 that the curious reproductive habits of ferns were explained—and then by an amateur. In that year a paper describing the process was published by Friedrich Wilhelm Benedikt Hofmeister, a nearsighted German bookseller who had solved the mystery after seven years of sparetime research (Hofmeister, a school dropout at age 14, was ultimately rewarded for his epochal discoveries with an appointment in 1863 as professor at the University of Heidelberg).

In place of the flowers, fruit and seeds that enable most plants to propagate themselves, ferns have spores, generally so inconspicuous they had been overlooked or misunderstood. Spores are tiny reproductive particles that grow into plants unlike the parent fern but containing sexual organs capable of producing new spore-bearing ferns. It is this two-stage sequence of reproduction—spore

(continued on page 17)

Identifying ferns by family

Walking through the woods, trying to recognize the ferns you see can be a frustrating experience, for many species differ in subtle details that may be discernible only to a botanist using a microscope. You can make a rough identification, however, because ferns are classified into botanical families. And although the definitions of the families are matter of scholarly dispute, all members of a single family share two distinctive characteristics: general growth habits and the patterns formed by sori— the clusters of tiny spore sacs (sporangia) that, on most ferns, are found on the undersides of the fronds.

These familial characteristics are illustrated in the following pictures of ferns that are representative of 17 families native to or commonly cultivated in the United States and Canada. The classification used—a specialized one different from those in general botanical references—was devised by J. A. Crabbe and A. C. Jermy of the British Museum and John Mickel of the New York Botanical Garden and modified by David B. Lellinger, curator of ferns at the Smithsonian Institution.

BOTRYCHIUM DISSECTUM
Cut-leaved grape fern

OPHIOGLOSSACEAE

The low-growing grape fern (left), typical of the Ophioglossaceae, is less than a foot tall. Its spores are borne in spherical spore cases (below), which are located on a separate stalk, technically a fertile part of the frond that rises from the base of the leafy sterile part.

MARSILEACEAE

Most Marsileaceae ferns have four-part fronds that resemble four-leaf clovers, and they float face up in still water. Although their short-stalked, hairy spore cases, near or at the bases of the fronds, are distinctive, the fiddleheads and clover-like fronds are identification enough.

MARSILEA VESTITA
Hairy pepperwort

OSMUNDACEAE

Like the royal fern (below), all Osmundaceae have separate clusters of spherical spore cases (right), bright green when young, darkening to brown. On the royal fern they are borne at the end of the stalklike frond; on other ferns of this family they spring from the middle of the frond.

OSMUNDA REGALIS
Royal fern

AZOLLACEAE

Called mosquito ferns and found floating in thick mats on still water, these ferns have as a distinguishing feature their rows of overlapping, oval leaves. These have dark green lobes at the water's surface, like the Mexican mosquito fern below, and nearly transparent submerged lobes.

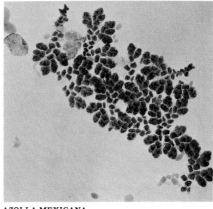

AZOLLA MEXICANA
Mexican mosquito fern

SALVINIACEAE

The small water spangles, which are found floating in still water, have pairs of hairy leaves and submerged third leaves, which produce, along their veins, hundreds of fine translucent hairs. These absorb nutrients for the plant, serving one of the various functions of true roots.

SALVINIA ROTUNDIFOLIA
Water spangles

VITTARIACEAE

The tropical shoestring ferns cascade down from the trunks of trees and can be easily identified by their drooping fronds, which are as slender and limp as their descriptive common name suggests. Their spore cases are hidden within the fronds in long grooves that run parallel to the edges of the fronds.

VITTARIA LINEATA
Shoestring fern

ADIANTACEAE

The ferns of this tropical and subtropical family vary greatly in appearance. They range from the billowing northern maidenhair to the wiry cliff brake. But the spore cases of most of these ferns are borne in a distinctive pattern. As shown in the two close-ups beneath the ferns, the cases rim the edge of the frond and are covered by its edge, which curls over to form a protective envelope.

PELLAEA ATROPURPUREA
Purple cliff brake

ADIANTUM PEDATUM
Northern maidenhair

LYGODIUM PALMATUM
Hartford fern

SCHIZAECEAE

Although members of this family can have habits of growth as different as the vinelike climbing Hartford fern and the rare low-growing curly-grass fern, they all have similar spore cases that are roughly oval in shape. Those of the climbing fern are borne under a scalelike covering on finely divided leaflets near the tip of the long, twining frond; those of the curly-grass fern are found at the tip of an otherwise bare stalk.

SCHIZAEA PUSILLA
Curly-grass fern

PARKERIACEAE

The ferns that make up this family are found in still water, submerged or on the surface, rooted in mud or afloat. Like the water fern shown, they typically have broad, sterile fronds at the base and a feathery canopy of finely divided fertile fronds whose blades curl under along both edges to enclose rows of spore cases beneath.

CERATOPTERIS PTERIDOIDES
American water fern

HYMENOPHYLLACEAE

Spreading like a carpet over or under rocks, as below, on trees, stream banks or behind waterfalls, the filmy ferns are recognizable by their small, thin fronds, which are only one cell thick. These delicate fronds are usually dense and overlapping and frequently are translucent.

TRICHOMANES PETERSII
Filmy fern

CYATHEACEAE

The unmistakable tree ferns have trunks and grow as tall as 50 feet, although their average height is 2 to 8 feet. The fronds are usually finely divided and spread in a crown at the top of the trunk, which is covered with the bases of old fronds and often overlaid with tough roots.

DICKSONIA SQUARROSA
Rough tree fern

PTERIDACEAE

The spore cases of the western bracken and all of its relatives lie beneath the turned-under edges of the leaves. On the western bracken this border is continuous (right), outlining the underside of the entire leaf, but on most members of the Pteridaceae family the border is discontinuous.

PTERIDIUM AQUILINUM
Western bracken

ATHYRIUM ASPLENIOIDES
Southern lady fern

ASPLENIACEAE

Although southern lady fern, maidenhair spleenwort and coastal wood fern all have clusters of spore cases that differ in shape, these clusters usually straddle veins on the undersides of the fronds. As seen in the close-ups, those of the southern lady fern are hook shaped, the spleenwort's are oblong and the wood fern's are kidney shaped.

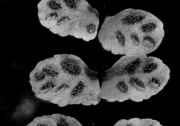

ASPLENIUM TRICHOMANES
Maidenhair spleenwort

DRYOPTERIS ARGUTA
Coastal wood fern

BLECHNACEAE

The many species of chain ferns around the world—European, Asian, American—all resemble the giant chain fern in appearance and are distinguished by covered oblong clusters of spore cases lying end to end along the midribs on the undersides of the fronds (below).

WOODWARDIA FIMBRIATA
Giant chain fern

OLEANDRACEAE

The stalwart sword fern and its relatives, which include the popular Boston fern, grow upright or drooping, singly or in clumps in warm climates. They bear clusters of round spore cases beneath kidney-shaped membranes that march in regular rows near the edges of leaflets on the undersides of the fronds.

POLYPODIACEAE

The polypodies include both the tidy American wall fern (left) and the sprawling tropical staghorn. Their spore cases lack the usual membrane covering and are generally found at the end of a vein branch on the underside of the frond.

POLYPODIUM VIRGINIANUM
American wall fern

NEPHROLEPIS CORDIFOLIA
Tuber sword fern

DAVALLIACEAE

The bear's-foot fern and its relatives live on tree trunks with their scaly rhizomes, the thickened stems, exposed to the air. Most of these ferns have feathery fronds and their distinctive spore case coverings open toward the edges of the fronds.

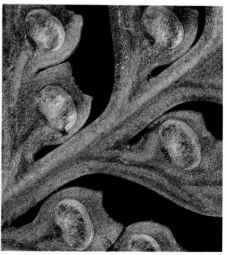

HUMATA TYERMANNII
Bear's-foot fern

to sexual plant, sexual plant to fern—that Hofmeister recognized.

Fern spores are dustlike. They are hidden on the underside of the fronds, in cases called sporangia. One sporangium may contain hundreds of spores, and each fern may bear thousands of sporangia, which are clustered in bunches called sori, creating shapes of great beauty and variety. The sori of the *Hemionitis arifolia,* for example, form a delicate rust-colored network along the veins of the fertile fronds.

As the sporangia mature, they burst and scatter the spores. Since most ferns are found in moist places, the spore may land on soil wet enough for it to germinate, though a capricious wind may blow it to a place that is too dry or too shady for germination. Assuming that no such calamities occur, the spore will put out a chain of cells in a few days. In a few months these cells produce a heart-shaped quarter-inch plant. This is not the new fern, but the prothallium, or sexual generation, which will actually produce the new fern. This tiny plant is a hermaphrodite, bearing male and female organs, and containing the seeds of its own destruction.

The sexual organs of the prothallium, in true fern fashion, are concealed on its underside. The male parts, or antheridia, contain the sperm and are located at the base of the plant; the female components, or archegonia, harbor the eggs and are at the opposite notched end. A film created on the prothallium by a droplet of rain is sufficient to enable the sperm to swim to the egg and fertilize it. (Since there can be no sperm swimming around without sufficient moisture, it is evident that ferns can reproduce copiously only in wet environments.)

The fertilized egg cell divides and produces the sporophyte— the familiar fern capable of bearing spores. As the sporophyte matures, the prothallium withers and eventually dies. (If the prothallium's sexual organs have not succeeded in effecting fertilization, they have at least succeeded in postponing its death, since it lives until it does produce a sporophyte.) The average time that is needed to produce a recognizable fern from a spore is about the same as that required by human beings to reproduce by their more direct method: nine months.

Circuitous though this reproductive process may be, the fern has survived and thrived in great variety. The color green is almost synonymous in most people's minds with the word fern, and indeed most ferns *are* green. There are some notable exceptions, such as the pink, or rosy, maidenhair, whose young fronds are suffused with a delicate blush; as the fronds mature, their background color changes from a pale to a medium green. Several fern species have dramatic white markings, among them a variety of the Cretan brake fern *(Pteris cretica albo-lineata),* which has a creamy white stripe running down the center of each dark green leaflet. The most unusually colored ferns are the *Pityrogramma,* which have either gold or silver undersides.

Nowhere is the variety assumed by ferns more evident than in the tropics, where they persist in staggering diversity. Ferns are most abundant in the highlands of equatorial regions, where fog-shrouded mountain slopes supply ideal growing conditions. (They have been found at altitudes as high as 16,000 feet.) The tree ferns, of which there are some 700 species (there are 10,000 known fern species in all, and 7,500 of them are tropical), attain a height of 50 feet and a spread of 20 feet in Australia and New Zealand. From a distance they look more like palms than ferns. The trunks of the tree ferns are interestingly varied. The Australian species generally have scaly coverings on their trunks, whereas those of the Hawaiian species tend to be covered with soft blond hairs.

THE SMALLEST GENUS   The tree ferns are as large as a modern fern can get: their antithesis is the filmy fern, which is so tiny that a whole colony might be found under an ordinary tree leaf. It is also so fragile that the fronds are sometimes only a single cell thick; the fine print on a legal contract might be read through one of these fronds. Despite their delicacy, filmy ferns have been known to live as long as 10 years in cultivation, though their need for humidity is so great that some of them can be kept alive only by floating them in water. There are also true water ferns, which grow so readily under or on water that they can become a weed.

There are ferns that climb, too, sometimes as much as 30 feet. The lygodiums comprise 45 species, of which the Japanese climbing fern is the best known. Most of these are tropical, but the Japanese climbing fern is subtropical and can be grown in the southern United States. The Hartford climbing fern is hardy as far north as Massachusetts, and was once common in Connecticut, where it picked up its name. However, it was so devastated by indiscriminate plucking during one of the few American manifestations of the British fern mania that in 1869 the Connecticut legislature passed a law protecting it.

A WIDE DISTRIBUTION   Ferns are found everywhere except areas covered by ice the year round. Though this leaves out the polar regions, over 500 species eke out an existence in the seemingly inhospitable Arctic, where they have developed tissue-thin leaves to make the most of the sparse sunshine.

Desert species of ferns account for roughly the same number

(continued on page 22)

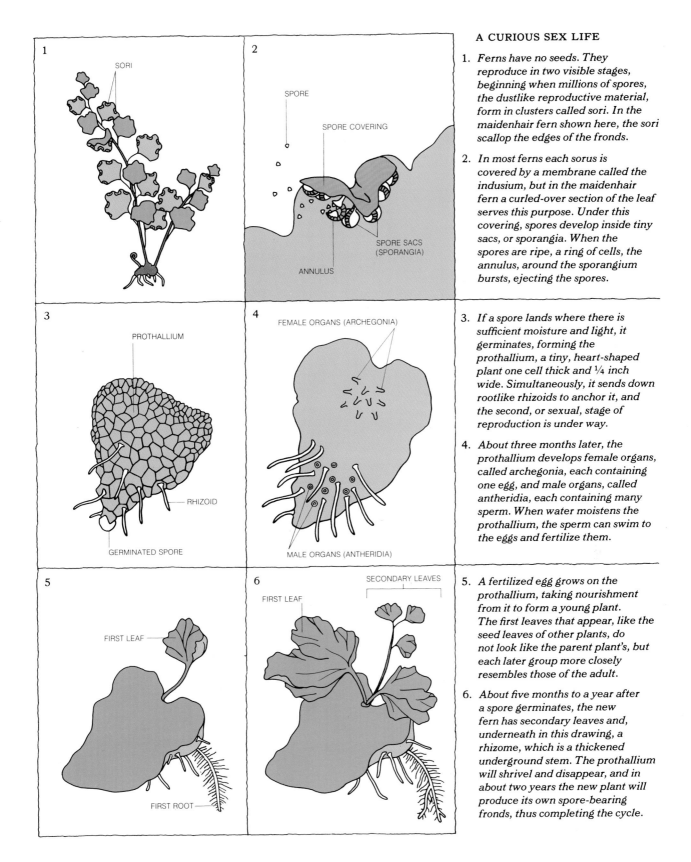

A CURIOUS SEX LIFE

1. *Ferns have no seeds. They reproduce in two visible stages, beginning when millions of spores, the dustlike reproductive material, form in clusters called sori. In the maidenhair fern shown here, the sori scallop the edges of the fronds.*

2. *In most ferns each sorus is covered by a membrane called the indusium, but in the maidenhair fern a curled-over section of the leaf serves this purpose. Under this covering, spores develop inside tiny sacs, or sporangia. When the spores are ripe, a ring of cells, the annulus, around the sporangium bursts, ejecting the spores.*

3. *If a spore lands where there is sufficient moisture and light, it germinates, forming the prothallium, a tiny, heart-shaped plant one cell thick and ¼ inch wide. Simultaneously, it sends down rootlike rhizoids to anchor it, and the second, or sexual, stage of reproduction is under way.*

4. *About three months later, the prothallium develops female organs, called archegonia, each containing one egg, and male organs, called antheridia, each containing many sperm. When water moistens the prothallium, the sperm can swim to the eggs and fertilize them.*

5. *A fertilized egg grows on the prothallium, taking nourishment from it to form a young plant. The first leaves that appear, like the seed leaves of other plants, do not look like the parent plant's, but each later group more closely resembles those of the adult.*

6. *About five months to a year after a spore germinates, the new fern has secondary leaves and, underneath in this drawing, a rhizome, which is a thickened underground stem. The prothallium will shrivel and disappear, and in about two years the new plant will produce its own spore-bearing fronds, thus completing the cycle.*

The translucent fronds of a Hymenophyllum polyanthos, a filmy fern native to the tropics, rest on a safari member's hand. Back home, the fern was later planted in moss in the shelter of a terrarium.

A hunt for the exotic

Slogging through the humid, insect-ridden undergrowth of a tropical rain forest is not most people's idea of fun. But to 13 members of a Florida fern society a five-day fern-hunting expedition to the West Indian island of Dominica was rewarding, for they returned home with plants as varied as the tiny, filmy fern shown at left and a massive elephant's-ear fern with broad fronds up to 2 feet long.

Carrying the plant-importing permits required by the U.S. Department of Agriculture, the fern hunters traveled to a remote location in the Dominican interior, 3,000 feet above sea level. Armed with trowel, knife, collecting bag and a lunch of bananas and native bread, they followed mountain streams to collect choice plants and spores, then trudged back to prepare their treasures for the trip home.

In a cooperative effort, fern hunters take advantage of a clear, rushing stream to wash their plants and remove excess dirt, to lighten the load in their plastic collecting bags. The sight and sound of the running water also helped the group to navigate through the dense tropical forest.

Hiking along a sunny stretch of the many miles of stream bed the fern hunters explored, safari leader Bill Hemmer passes a stand of young tree ferns (far right), and Thelypteris (just behind him) while he scans other tropical ferns for unusual specimens to take home. Despite the heat, Hemmer wore heavy shoes and overalls for protection in the rocky, wet terrain.

After clipping off fronds, which could bear pests, Bill Hemmer places each plant in a separate plastic bag. That way, if U.S. Customs inspectors had found an undesirable insect or fungus on a plant, they could easily separate it from the others for fumigation.

IMPORTING FERNS

Vacationers in tropical lands may bring spores of exotic ferns into the U.S.— and the ferns themselves if they are free of soil, pests and disease and are packed in materials such as uncut sphagnum moss or excelsior. A permit is needed even for small quantities, and the imports must be declared on a customs declaration form. For more information on what may be imported, a booklet may be obtained by sending a request to Travelers Tips, Department of Agriculture, Washington, D.C. 20250.

as arctic ferns, an astonishingly large total considering that ferns cannot reproduce without moisture. They are as wide ranging as their arctic counterparts, and are particularly abundant in the southwestern United States. Many desert ferns grow under rocks, where there is life-giving coolness, developing coverings of hair and scales to conserve the scant moisture available to them.

Sunny Jamaica has the greatest concentration of fern species in the world—there are over 500 on this Connecticut-sized Caribbean island (4,500 square miles). By comparison, the entire United States has only 250 species, and 107 of those are found in Florida, which may have been the first stop on a wind-borne odyssey that began somewhere in the Caribbean.

Fifteen per cent of all ferns are native to temperate regions, including most of those growing in backyards and forests. American gardeners generally make their choices from this group, and since it numbers 1,500 species the possibilities for an interesting fern garden anywhere in the country are practically unlimited. Even for gardeners who live where the winters are long and hard, there is a subdivision of the temperate group called the alpine fern, which brings a touch of mountain greenery even to climate Zone 3.

On the other hand, those smitten in the tropics with the delicate beauty of the water clover fern *(Marsilea minuta),* a bog plant with a dozen or so blades that look like tiny four-leaf clovers, should not despair when they return north. It has a hardy twin, the *Marsilea quadrifola,* that can be kept outdoors in Zones 4 to 8. It also is unnecessary to convert one's home into a rain forest simply because a tropical fern has been acquired for a house plant. These ferns generally do best with a humidity of around 70 per cent, but since most people are unable and unwilling to live under greenhouse conditions, a realistically attainable figure, around 50 per cent, is a happy medium for man and fern alike.

If the humidity around the ferns is high enough, the chances are good that they will live up to their reputation of being generally easy to grow. Under these conditions they are usually pest-free.

DEALING WITH PESTS

But even the most careful gardener and the healthiest fern have to contend with bugs sooner or later, indoors or out. A fern's worst enemy is the mealy bug, whose sweet secretions attract other insects. Ants feed on the mealy bug's secretions, carrying the bug to more distant parts of the fern; and fungi begin to grow in the secretions. (Mealy bugs look like tiny tufts of cotton, and feel like cotton tufts if you pick them off with your fingers.) Another pest, the aphid, or plant louse, sucks the sap out of ferns the same way that a mealy bug does. At first glance, the aphid looks like a tiny black or green seed kernel and it may go unnoticed unless the ferns receive a particularly thorough inspection.

To deal with any of these pests, try hosing down the plant with a stream of water strong enough to wash off insects but gentle enough not to harm the fern. If this does not work, a very mild solution of soap suds should be sprayed onto the plant. Do not use any chemical sprays on ferns except in cases of utter desperation, since many house ferns are so susceptible to chemical poisoning that they may be eradicated along with the bugs.

There are other unwelcome visitors that must be picked off by hand, such as scale, which looks like a tiny brown husk, and—like mealy bugs and aphids—will drain a plant of its sap. If a frond is heavily infested, the best thing to do is to cut it off and burn it. (Scales resemble sori, but their pattern is never of the same regularity; do not destroy a healthy frond without being sure that what looked like scale at first glance still looks like it at second.)

Snails and slugs (snails without shells) also will nibble on fern fronds outdoors. They come up onto the plant only at night, but if you see slimy trails around your ferns, you can be sure there are slugs nearby. (The Victorians used to lure snails and slugs out of hiding with heaps of bran and hops placed nearby.)

VICTORIAN REMEDIES

Fern fanciers a century ago also were troubled by caterpillars, which they hunted at night with kerosene lamps. And crickets, despite their Oriental reputations as talismans of good luck and providers of pleasant music, were lured to their deaths in beetle traps by the Victorians, who valued their ferns more. Weevils, or snout beetles, also were a major problem then—they are not today because natural selection tends to weed out plants that cannot resist pests—and were driven out in a highly organized ritual akin to an exorcism. By day, sheets of white paper were placed under the afflicted ferns and smeared with an adhesive such as paste or tar. After nightfall, the weevil hunter stealthily entered the darkened room and suddenly turned a light upon the possessed plants, "at the same time giving them a shake," as an old account puts it. The beetles fell onto the paper and got stuck in the glue, which held them until they could be disposed of conveniently.

SPLENDID SIMPLICITY

The Victorians' quaint methods of pest control must have been quite an adventure in themselves. But now—as then—growing ferns is the real adventure: for the beginning gardener who hangs a Boston fern in the living room, as well as for the veteran who has nurtured a variety of species into a cascading garden. They share the simple splendor that the fern can bring, and the feeling of a place in the woods that even a few ferns can give.

A feathery touch for the garden 2

The commanding advantage of ferns for the outdoor garden is their ability to thrive in places where other plants will not even survive. They are a fine solution for the problem areas that exist in almost every yard. Most grow in shade, in acid soil, in moist but well-drained land (although there are also ferns for sunny, dry, alkaline places). And some are uniquely adapted to rocky slopes that seem inhospitable to anything but weeds.

Yet ferns ought not be considered the last desperate choice after every other garden plant has failed. Their woodsy attractiveness is a delight anywhere. And they fill a number of purposes in the landscape, providing beds of uncommon variety, serving as background plantings, dividing one area from another, framing pools, even making unusually pleasant boundary fences.

Before you plant your first ferns, it is a good idea to make a rough scale drawing of your property to get an idea of the area available. Allow at least 2 square feet of growing space for each fern—the small ones you start with will not stay that way. And you can always add to an underachieving planting. Mies van der Rohe's celebrated dictum that "less is more" is as applicable to growing ferns as it is to architecture.

In selecting a location for your ferns, look first for shade, since most of these plants are adapted to forest life. Around most suburban homes, the backyard and lawn will have many shaded areas where it is difficult to grow most plants. Allowing for the shadow cast by the house, which will usually occupy most of the width of the lot if not its length, and neighboring houses, to say nothing of a few trees, fences, garages and sheds, it becomes apparent that there is a great deal of space that is well suited to the culture of ferns and very little else.

Though ferns need less light than most other plants, they often need more water. If your garden has a low-lying area, that is

Lacy mountain wood fern (foreground) and northern lady fern frame a patch of delicate wildflowers—white Canada violets, pink columbine and yellow lady's slipper— in a border planting in New England.

25

probably the best place for ferns because it will catch water runoff and retain moisture longer. It is also wise to plant ferns in an area protected from wind. The best-protected areas are close to the house, at the base of a slope, or next to a fence or wall.

But do not give up on ferns if there are no shaded areas in your yard. Some ferns will grow in direct sunlight if you bear in mind that they are not cacti and need a watchful eye kept on their constant need for moisture and humidity. The lady fern is tolerant of the sun and is surprisingly hardy despite its delicate, gently textured fronds. Another interesting possibility for the shadeless garden is the Japanese climbing fern, which will clamber merrily up a sunny wall in the subtropics.

CHOOSING SPECIES TO GROW

The kinds of ferns you can plant depend on where you live, although even in the North, tropical species can be enjoyed outdoors if you grow them in pots and move them indoors for the winter. In the spring when all danger of frost has passed (*page 147*), sink the pots to their rims in soil and enjoy the ferns outdoors all summer and into the fall; in late autumn, take them up and bring them indoors. But since there are hundreds of hardy ferns, northern gardeners are not restricted by their harsh climates. It is rather like realizing that although you cannot grow a palm tree on your front lawn, a majestic pine tree has merits of its own.

The encyclopedia (*Chapter 5*) and the zone map appearing on page 146 indicate which species grow where. It must be remembered, however, that the zone divisions are not hard and fast, but only general, and there is plenty of room within them for differences of opinion and experience. Elevated areas in the South, for example, will have cooler temperatures than those that are low lying, as will those in Hawaii, which is otherwise similar to southern Florida in its hospitality to tropical ferns.

For the adventurous gardener, there is always the possibility of breaking out of rigid categories by taking a chance. The southern maidenhair fern, for example, makes forays into Missouri and western South Dakota, and with a little additional help might be able to survive in sheltered areas in gardens north of Virginia, which is generally its uppermost limit in the East. A judicious banking of soil around it, to give it protection from the harshest nights of winter, might enable a Yankee to enjoy its pale evergreen fronds as they flutter on their dark stalks.

If you live in the Deep South or the Southwest, ferns such as the Cretan brake, with its rippling fronds, and the aforementioned southern maidenhair, whose fronds look as though they have been edged with pinking shears, will meet the requirements of your climate. Both of these ferns can survive a flirtation with frost, but not an extended relationship with it, and generally they should not be grown in areas where the night temperature remains below 40° for any long period of time.

The maidenhair genus is so large (200 species) and so varied that you can have some of its members around no matter where you live, even if you do not put a southern maidenhair out in your northern backyard. A sure bet for a cold climate is *Adiantum pedatum,* or northern maidenhair. Linnaeus, the great Swedish botanist who devised the modern system of classifying plants by generic and specific names, thought it resembled a bird's foot, and thus christened it *pedatum.* To some it is known as the five-finger fern; to others it looks most like a fan of pale green ostrich plumes arising from a purple-black handle. It is tenacious enough to survive without special care as far north as Zone 4. Its height varies between 1 and 2 feet, and it needs continuous moisture in both hot and cold weather.

The genus *Dryopteris* (150 species) also provides many possibilities for the northern gardener. One of the most interesting is *D. goldiana* (Goldie's fern, which can grow as tall as 5 feet). Its fronds often are as much as a foot wide, so be sure to allow plenty of space for a Goldie's fern. The fronds are absent in winter, but in their growing season their leathery look is so handsome it more than compensates for the later absence. A half-sized relative, the evergreen shield fern, hangs on to its more modest fronds all year, and, planted near a Goldie's fern, will inspire thoughts of spring.

A numerically tiny but extremely useful genus of large ferns for the northern garden is *Osmunda,* whose aristocratic species number only 10. But among those 10 are such established favorites as the cinnamon and royal ferns and the interrupted fern, whose fertile fronds turn brown and wither in the middle, literally interrupting the otherwise orderly march of green pinnae, or leaflets, along the fronds' stalks.

Fern lovers in the southern half of the United States—where the climate is neither subtropical nor downright cold—have some fascinating opportunities to expand their gardens. There are 250 members of the genus *Pteris,* for example. And though all are from tropical or subtropical regions, many travel well.

Though more diminutive than the *Pteris,* the 80 species of the *Pellaea* genus include ferns of singular form that can add much charm to a garden in a mild climate. A perennial favorite is the New Zealand cliff brake, also known as the button fern because each frond looks like a double row of shiny green buttons hanging from a thick brown thread. An interesting companion to this fern is the Australian cliff brake, which has elongated oval or tapering, rather than round, buttons.

Fern gardeners who live in the warmest parts of the country—southern Florida, Southern California and parts of the Southwest—are limited only by the size of their yards, since they can choose among the thousands of varieties of ferns that require tropical or semitropical temperatures.

SELECTING A PLANT

When you go to a nursery to make your choice, choose a fern the same way you select fresh fruit at the market. Look for a specimen with good shape and color. Check carefully for pests, but remember that a pest-free plant is not necessarily healthy. Color that is too pale for the species, an unusual amount of browning, and fronds that have lost too many of their leaflets can all be indications of potential trouble.

You also should select your ferns with an eye to their eventual appearance on your property, and not just the sight they present at the nursery. Most ferns blend well with one another, but there is no point in having a 4-foot-high cinnamon fern growing next to a 5-foot-high Goldie's fern simply because they are both available. A pair of marginal wood ferns, less than half the height of the others, might be more in keeping with the scale and design of your garden and just as readily available.

Whether or not you want your ferns to multiply also should be an important part of your garden planning. Ferns such as the marginal wood fern, with a single crown of leaves—a vertically growing stem from which young fronds sprout—generally remain single plants. Those such as the hay-scented fern, with branching rhizomes—rootlike stems that grow horizontally under the ground and send up new fronds as they wander into new territory—multiply very rapidly. In any event, do not plant such nomadic ferns near property boundary lines unless your neighbor's taste in ferns coincides with yours.

MOVING WILD FERNS

The nursery is not the only source of new plants, of course. Many fern fanciers are tempted to supplement their gardens with wild plants, perhaps feeling about ferns as poet Thomas Gray did about flowers—that they were not born to blush unseen. But it usually is better to admire the wild plant in its natural habitat and leave it undisturbed.

More than 2,000 species of plants, including some ferns, were catalogued in 1975 by the Smithsonian Institution as "endangered, threatened, or recently extinct." Scott's spleenwort, always rare, is threatened with extinction in five states. And visitors to Onondaga and Madison counties in New York State should not move the hart's-tongue fern, which is native only to these two places in the United States. It is protected by state law. In fact, in many other areas it is against the law to dig up any plant growing on public land, including the ditches alongside roads.

But if you should come across a wild fern that catches your eye—and if you have permission to move it—the most compassionate method is to remove only a spore-bearing frond and raise your own (page 85). In the case of large ferns, only a few pinnae are necessary. Most fern spores are ripe for collection from late spring to late summer, which is when most collectors will be out wandering in the woods anyway. Another relatively harmless method of

As the center of a cinnamon fern dies, its progeny spread outward, forming a "fairy ring" of fiddleheads.

gathering ferns is to take only one of many growing tips from a clump or wandering rhizome characteristic of many ferns. Such cutting is most successful in early spring, before the new crosiers have begun to emerge. Where the fern reproduces by growing a bud at its leaf tip, for example, as the walking fern does, cut the tip of the mother frond as closely as possible to the bud, and remove only the bud from the soil.

If you are going to collect ferns by taking a bit of the clump or rhizome, carry a canteen of water and pour the water around the base of the fern before you cut; this will help hold the soil around the roots and prevent unnecessary violence to the separated portion of the plant. Cut cleanly through the rhizome with a sharp knife, and try to take as much soil as possible to minimize the inevitable shock. Wrap your prize in wet paper towels or pop it into a plastic bag, and do not dally on the way home. The sooner you replant it the better its chances of survival. But note that the rate of failure in transplanting from the wild is far higher than in transplanting cultivated ferns.

The new arrivals should be planted to the same depth you found them in, and in conditions as close as possible to the ones in which they originally grew. Use stakes for large cuttings and cut

DIVIDING BRANCHING RHIZOMES

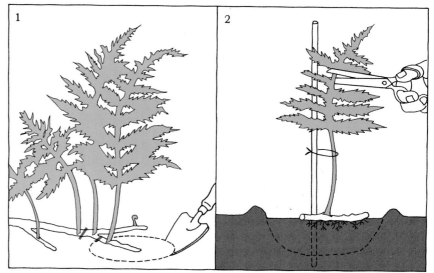

Ferns that spread by means of branching rhizomes can be divided (red bars) if a growing tip is left for the parent. Use a sharp knife to cut a frond-bearing branch at least 2 inches long, then dig it up with enough soil to protect the roots.

Replant the rhizome section at the depth it had been growing; it will spread in the direction the growing tip points. Stake the frond and trim off the top half to lessen the amount of water and food the rhizome must supply. Firm the soil and water it well.

back any broken and badly wilted fronds to help compensate for the roots that were cut off.

Although some authorities hold that fall is the best time for transplanting ferns, since there is then less possibility of disturbance to their growth and the completion of their cycle, most gardeners prefer spring, perhaps as much for their own psyches as for the plants themselves. It is the time closest to the appearance of unfurling crosiers, and the time when the gardener himself, after a dark winter spent indoors, rushes out to his reborn hobby with renewed energy. Ferns are so accommodating that almost any time except the dead of winter will do.

SOIL PREPARATION

You can get a head start on helping your plants make the transition into your garden—whether they come from the nursery or from the wild—by preparing the soil beforehand. If there is a shady corner of the yard where the leaves have a tendency to pile up despite your best efforts, that area is the ideal site for a fernery, since a good supply of leaf mold is the chief requirement for the perfect fern soil (although peat moss is a fair substitute). Leaf mold is the decomposed matter of the forest and can include any plant debris that would be at home in the deep woods but out of place in a conventionally tidy garden: twigs, pine needles, even fruit—all of

DIVIDING A NONBRANCHING RHIZOME

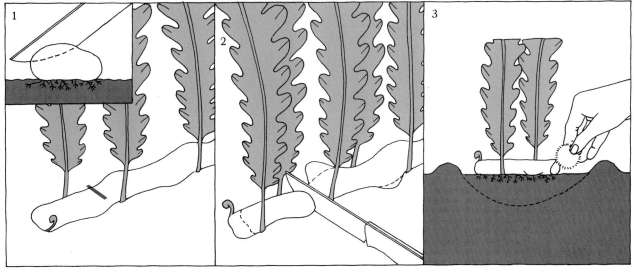

A fern with a creeping rhizome that has a single growing tip can be divided, but only at some risk to the parent. Force the rhizome to branch by cutting halfway through it (inset) at a point (red bar) just beyond a swelling that indicates a bud.

In about two months, when the side bud has rooted and is at least 1 inch long, while the growing tip is at least 2 inches long, sever the tip by completing the partial cut. Use a hand trowel to gently dig up the tip, its roots and a generous soil ball.

Replant the severed tip immediately in its new bed at the depth it was previously growing. Pour water over the cut ends of both plants to clean them and dust with a fungicide applied with a cotton ball. Firm the soil around both plants and water.

the things that make an autumn stroll through the woods such a delight as your feet bounce merrily over the spongy evidence of nature's unsightly but knowing housekeeping.

You can speed the process of turning fallen leaves into leaf mold by chopping them up with a power mower and putting them in a container of wire mesh about 3 feet across and 3 feet high. Most leaves are slightly acid or neutral, but leaf mold can be made more acid, to satisfy the needs of most ferns, with the leaves of oaks, beeches, blueberries or deciduous azaleas. To lessen the acidity for certain ferns, simply add ground limestone. The leaf mold will loosen the soil and permit good drainage, particularly important if it is a compacted tree-shaded area where the soil has been subjected to heavy demands by tree roots. A good soil mix for outdoor ferns calls for 2 parts leaf mold (or peat moss) and sharp builder's sand added to 1 part garden loam. A depth of 12 inches will be needed by most ferns, even though they are shallow rooted, as the soil tends to pack down with repeated watering.

A soil well laced with leaf mold generally will be sufficiently acid to satisfy the acid requirements of the woodland ferns that most gardeners grow. However, the only way to be sure is to check.

THE pH SOIL TEST   One way to tell whether your soil is too acid or alkaline is to observe the appearance of your ferns—growth will be stunted and some mature fronds will drop off. But it is better to find out if there is a problem before such symptoms appear by testing the pH, or relative abundance of free hydrogen atoms, in the soil. The test, which is performed with an inexpensive kit, is simplicity itself: strips of paper are dipped into a moist soil sample and the colors that they turn are matched to those in an instruction sheet. (Plant lovers are indebted to a Danish scientist named Sorensen for the devising of this organic method of monitoring the growing medium of one plant with the by-product of another; the paper that is used in the basic test is made from coloring matter obtained from lichens.) The entire range of the pH scale is 1 to 14, with 7, right in the middle, representing a neutral soil, readings down from it representing increasing acidity and results upward from 7 indicating increasing alkalinity. Some papers test for specific points within the entire possible range and are of interest only if you have a species that requires an acidity of absolutely 4.5 and not one whit more or less, an event of extremely unlikely occurrence.

Most woodland ferns do best in an acid soil with a pH of 5.5 to 6.5; those that prefer alkalinity, at home among limestone rocks or in desert regions, need a pH of 7.0 to 8.0. If your soil is too acid, you can move it toward alkalinity by adding ground limestone, an ounce at a time per cubic foot of soil, allowing it to work for a week and then retesting until the desired level is reached. You can amend a too-alkaline soil the same way with ground sulfur, using only one fifth of an ounce per cubic foot of soil.

But do not attempt to change the pH very much; the amendment will be short lived—a year or two at best. You would be better off to select ferns that are compatible with the existing chemistry of your soil. There are plenty of choices for acid conditions, and although ferns that prefer an alkaline soil are far fewer in number, some are common, and you should try at least one of them—such as the purple cliff brake, *Pellaea atropurpurea*, with its muted shadings of brown, blue and purple. Since it grows in limestone cliffs all over the country, it will be most at home in a soil laced with crushed limestone or oyster shells.

TRANSPLANTS FROM POTS

Once the soil has been prepared, it is time for the delicate task of transplanting the fern from the container it came in to its new home. Wet the soil in the container thoroughly so as much of it as possible will adhere to the roots when the plant is removed. Replant the fern to the same depth as it was in its nursery container. Except for a tree fern, a fern with a crown is ideally planted so that its stem is fully covered but its tip is exposed. Wandering ferns should be planted at the depth at which they were previously

PROPAGATING A WALKING FERN

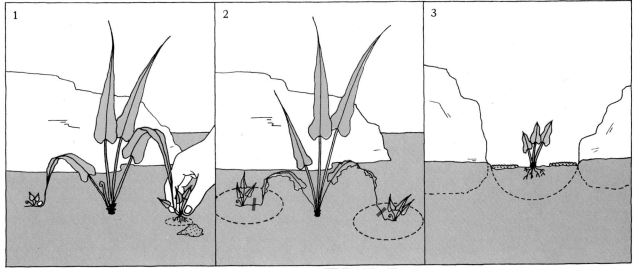

To create new ferns from plantlets that develop on the tips of some fronds, bend such a frond to the ground in the shade of the parent. Plant the bud where it touches, anchoring it with a pebble; if it has roots, bury them.

Two to six months later, when the bud is well rooted, sever the connecting frond, which may have withered. Cut ½ inch from the tip (red bars). Dig up the bud (dotted lines) and, if the new bed is far away, bag it in plastic.

Set the bud in a prepared bed, pressing down on the soil to create a slight saucer. Provide shade by embedding several rocks—preferably limestone—nearby. Then, if moss is available, place some in the saucer as mulch.

A scientist's surprising acid test

After many years of mixing potting soil by feel, adding a pinch of bone meal as fertilizer, a bit of limestone for alkalinity, and a handful of leaf mold for acidity, Dr. Bruce McAlpin, fern horticulturist at the New York Botanical Garden, became curious about the specific effect of those ingredients on the acidity of his basic soil mixtures. To find out, he mixed a quart each of two basic planting mixes. For one quart he used 1 part garden loam, 1 part builder's sand and 2 parts leaf mold; the mixture tested out at pH 6.8, or almost neutral. For the other he substituted sphagnum peat moss for the leaf mold, giving the mixture a slightly acid pH of 6.0. (A pH test at a different location, McAlpin warned, might yield different results, since garden loam, leaf mold and peat moss all can have different levels of acidity.)

McAlpin divided each quart of basic mix into four portions, added a measured amount of bone meal or limestone to each, and tested each portion. The resulting data, shown in the table below, included some surprises. For example, a tablespoon of bone meal, a fertilizer that is usually considered to be an inert, neutral substance, raised the pH rating of the peat moss mixture almost a full point, while limestone, which is usually added specifically to increase the degree of alkalinity, raised the pH level of the same mixture only two tenths of a point.

While the figures might appear to indicate that bone meal could be substituted for limestone, the two are not really interchangeable. Bone meal, besides being at least 10 times more expensive than limestone, is a root-building fertilizer that dissolves in the soil, is absorbed by the plant and needs to be replenished each year. Limestone remains an undissolved part of the soil mixture for much longer and needs to be replenished only once every three or four years. The study does indicate, however, that it is wise to check the pH rating of soil after the addition of any one of these elements.

While McAlpin, the scientist, thought the test results had significance, McAlpin, the gardener, admitted he continued to mix his potting soil by feel.

ONE QUART OF BASIC MIX WITH LEAF MOLD = pH 6.8	ONE QUART OF BASIC MIX WITH PEAT MOSS = pH 6.0
plus 1 tablespoon limestone = pH 7.03	plus 1 tablespoon limestone = pH 6.2
plus 2 tablespoons limestone = pH 7.05	plus 2 tablespoons limestone = pH 6.8
plus 1 tablespoon bone meal = pH 7.1	plus 1 tablespoon bone meal = pH 6.9
plus 2 tablespoons bone meal = pH 7.1	plus 2 tablespoons bone meal = pH 7.0

growing. Those with underground rhizomes should be planted shallowly, with the rhizomes no more than an inch below the soil.

If the soil in your garden is poorly drained, put a few stones or slates in the bottom of the planting hole. Pack the soil lightly around the roots—they need air as well as water—making sure that there are no large empty pockets where the roots can dry out. The roots should be carefully spread out in the planting hole, and not placed into the soil in a matted clump. This is less of a problem with a spreading rhizome, because the rhizome itself acts as a spacer for the roots.

Once you have planted your ferns, lay a hose on the ground so that a very gentle trickle of water can inundate the newly filled-in areas around their bases. In a new planting, let the water run until the ground feels thoroughly wet but is not on the verge of turning into a soggy mudbank. Succeeding waterings can be somewhat lighter, just enough to keep the soil constantly moist to the touch, but you will need to return to heavy soakings in the heat of summer. A gentle early-morning misting of the foliage during an especially dry period is wise as well as merciful, but it is kinder to skip misting entirely if you are prone to subject the ferns to a hurried ordeal under high water pressure. Use only the finest nozzle setting, or the lightest possible touch if pressure is effected by squeezing on a trigger.

PROVIDING MOISTURE

The newly planted fern garden will make few demands upon your time—just be careful that the earth supporting the ferns never becomes dry. The ferns themselves will tell you if they are receiving enough water—a high proportion of browning fronds on new growth is one signal, as is a generally drooping appearance. But do not wait for the plants to suffer, since it is easy to check the water in the soil around a fern. Poke a stick into the ground to a depth of about 6 inches, or perhaps a foot in the case of a large fern. The stick will be moist along its full length if your ferns are getting enough water. If the soil around your fern is really dry, a finger stuck into the earth will tell you even more quickly. The earth should be moist from the surface down; most ferns have such shallow roots that the presence of water at their lowest extremities may not be enough to tide them over.

After your ferns are settled in, there is no reason to fertilize them unless they seem off color—pale green or yellowed—or slow in growth. Since ferns yield neither fruit nor flower, there is little incentive to speed the growth. But if you should decide to add nutrients, do so twice a year, in spring and midsummer, using a fertilizer made of fish. The most direct—and the smelliest—way of

NUTRIENTS FROM FISH

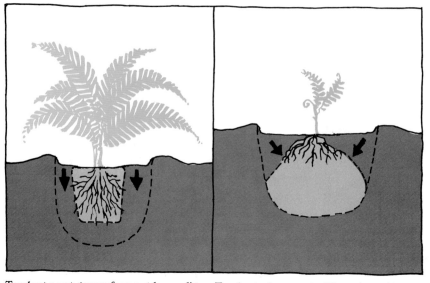

To plant a pot-grown fern outdoors, dig a roomy hole and set the root ball in at the same depth it previously grew at. Fill the hole, then press directly downward (arrows) to firm the soil and create an inch-deep saucer.

To plant a bare-rooted fern, drape it over a firm cone of soil. Fill the hole, and in this case press at an angle (arrows) to push the roots against the soil cone; if the roots are pressed directly downward, they might be torn.

getting the nutrients in the fish to help your ferns is to do as the Indians did, and bury the parts you cannot eat—bones, entrails and fins—in the soil at the base of the plant. Modern fish fertilizers do the job as well but have been deodorized. Some people use fish meal, which is simply ground-up dried fish; it is easily scattered around the ferns, and it does not have to be mixed with water before application. Others use a fish emulsion, a thick brown paste, in dosages half as strong as those recommended by the manufacturer. Dilute the emulsion with water (half a teaspoon for a quart of water is about right for the usual concentration that is marketed).

COLD-WEATHER SAFEGUARDS
But however splendidly your ferns grow, it is inevitable that, as the days of fall close in, some will begin to lose foliage. Some cold-weather protection generally must be arranged, even if the fern is considered fully hardy. Spent fronds should be left on the plants until spring, and additional leaves from other plants piled around the ferns as a mulch. Evergreen boughs make an excellent shoring for mulch, as do strips of bark. They also will keep your deciduous ferns from looking like part of a compost heap. If you grow evergreen ferns, they should not be smothered with leaves but can be given a light mulching. Even where severe cold is not a problem, it is advisable to put a slight covering of leaves over the fern bed as a precaution.

Come spring, all those leaves and branches will have to be cleared away. Do not lose any time in removing anything heavy that might cause a newborn crosier to be deformed or to snap in the effort to push itself up. But do not throw away that potentially beneficial organic matter, either. Just dump all but the evergreen boughs into the pile where you make leaf-mold compost—and soon you will have the essential ingredient for growing still more ferns.

These procedures should be followed whether you grow only a few ferns in a shady, moist part of your garden, as most people do, or become so enamored of these delicate plants that you make extensive use of them as dominant features of your land. They provide practical remedies for landscaping difficulties because they will grow in places that are ordinarily inhospitable to plant life and because, in many circumstances, they serve the purposes of customary plants that will not grow there.

A simple bed is the most practical way for the average gardener with limited space to enjoy ferns' gentle, only seemingly undisciplined beauty. The length of the bed can be whatever the size of your property allows and the width as narrow as 2 feet if the planting is to be confined to the smaller species. Stick to ferns with crowns if you wish to maintain any semblance of a planned growing area; ferns that reproduce by means of spreading rhizomes will soon obliterate any trace of order.

Tall ferns should be placed at the back of the bed and shorter ones at the front if you want to enjoy them when they reach their full size. For example, royal fern reaches an eventual height of around 5 feet, but it may be a third that size when you bring it home from the nursery. If you want it to stay small, keep the soil around it somewhat drier than it is for your other ferns. An evergreen shield fern is half the size of a royal when it is fully grown, and obviously should be planted in front of the royals if you want to be able to enjoy the sight of both ferns while sitting on your terrace or officiating at your barbecue. Both of these ferns are crown formers, and since they do not spread quickly, they are ideal choices for a fern bed.

Ferns planted together should be all acid- or all alkaline-soil types (the royal and the evergreen shield fern prefer acid soil) with similar moisture requirements. These are the two main considerations for keeping your ferns happy.

A bed of ferns, in addition to being a thing of beauty in itself, is an excellent camouflage for a sway-backed fence or an exposed cinder-block foundation. Since ferns are undemanding about the source of the shade they require, they will be as happy in the

PLANNING A FERN BED

shadow of a tree or shrub as they will be in the shade of a building. They are therefore ideal plants for use in the mixed planting where the taller components will cut off so much light that the use of most other greenery is precluded.

A particularly felicitous combination in a mixed planting includes ferns, azaleas and evergreens, since all three thrive in the same soil, acid-laden as it is sure to be from leaves and needles. Azaleas also share the ferns' tolerance of shady places, and the two would do well planted under an oak tree, another acid-lover (and acid provider, through oak-leaf mulch).

Some purists believe that only wildflowers should be planted with ferns, because they have the delicacy of proportion and tint that complement the same qualities in the fern. Any or all of a dozen members of the trillium family alone provide superb counterpoints for ferns in an informal woods planting.

There also is a large palette of more familiar and more spectacular flowers that will thrive in a fern bed. The tuberous begonia will be happy along the lightly shaded edges of your mixed planting and will reward you with the incredible diversity of the shapes it assumes. The tiger lily also will prosper in light shade, bursting forth with black-spotted orange blooms in late summer.

BUILDING A COBBLE Ferns' affinity for flowers is obvious, but ferns take on a different, craggy look when planted with rocks, a pairing as inevitable as corned beef and cabbage. "Cobbles," or hilly rock plantings, are a Yankee tradition, and the word cobble itself is an old American term for a rocky slope. A cobble can easily be constructed in a gently graded area of the garden by stripping off the soil and substituting a mixture of equal parts of loam and humus to which has been added slaked lime (about ¼ pound per square yard, and no more; this is strong stuff). Your new soil should be 10 to 12 inches deep. If you can get some chunks of tufa, a highly porous limestone, set them deeply into the soil. Field limestone is second choice; lacking that, chunks of concrete will do. Arrange your stones as naturally as possible, so that it seems that a more celestial hand than yours has put them there.

A limestone cobble is one place where you do not have to keep your ferns shaded, and it provides the perfect home away from home for the sun-loving, cliff-hanging cliff brakes. Though most of them are not hardy enough for northern cobbles, there are some that will survive even in Zone 3, including purple cliff brake and its similarly colored and only slightly smaller relative, Sierra cliff brake. Both tolerate shade, sun or drought.

An equally obliging addition to your cobble might be common

woodsia, which will also put up with either a sunny or shady spot. Its heart is really in the shade, though, where it will grow to a height of more than a foot and maintain a strong green color; in the sun, its foliage will be yellowish and the plant will be somewhat shorter. Walking fern is a fern of singular beauty for the shaded cobble. Its fronds, as much as a foot long, look like green arrow-heads, and the plant has a singular habit of growth, for it reproduces by probing into rock crevices with the tips of its fronds, from which new ferns emerge. It also reproduces in moss, so if you have a patch of it in your cobble, chances are good that you will soon have a colony of walking ferns. Some other good candidates for a cobble are the commonest of the spleenworts, the ebony, which is often found growing wild with the walking fern, and, if you can find one at a plant store, hart's-tongue, which has shiny green tongue-like fronds as long as two feet. This fern is rare in North America but widely grown in England.

ACID ROCKS

Several interesting rock-garden ferns are acid-lovers, and a cobble can be built for them using an acid soil mixture and acid rocks such as quartz, granite or slate instead of limestone. The parsley fern, which is never more than 5 inches tall and aptly resembles a sprig of flat parsley, would grace the acid rocks.

A cobble requires less watering than a fern bed, since water from its higher levels seeps into the soil and keeps it moist to a few inches below the surface. If the land is so smooth that even the gentlest of slopes would appear incongruous, a rock garden can be mounded, although it will not look as natural as a cobble would.

PLANTING AMONG COBBLES

1. *To make a fern rock garden, bury stones at least halfway in a sloping 12-inch bed of planting mix (page 38). Slant the stones down at the back to catch rain water. Plant ferns between them; add small stones to slow erosion.*

2. *To plant ferns in an existing wall of cobblestones, stuff crevices half full of planting mix. As you plant the ferns, shape the root balls to conform to the shapes of the crevices. Cover the soil with small stones to hold it in place.*

Large rocks, sunk halfway into the soil at its base, will shore up the mound, but they should be irregular in appearance to avoid the artificial effect common in such plantings. Another alternative is a rock garden that is basically a bed of soil decorated with rocks. The rocks should be placed as naturally as possible. Sink them completely in soil, then raise them slowly out of it while studying them from every angle, to determine how much of the rock surface should be exposed. The narrow strips of soil between the rocks provide hospitable ledges for rock ferns.

A BOG GARDEN OF FERNS

Where the ground is so flat that a heavy rain makes your garden look like a rice paddy, there are at least a half dozen ferns that can thrive in muddy conditions and turn an eyesore into an eye-pleasing fern bog. A fern bog grows best next to a pond and looks especially attractive there; designed and planted to follow its contours, the bog can appear to be part of the pond, with the ferns seemingly growing in it. However, the concrete lining of the ordinary garden pond tends to make nearby soil alkaline and therefore unsuitable for most bog ferns, which prefer a very acid soil. To get around this problem for a fern bog adjoining concrete, scatter acid rocks along the edges of the bog to increase the acidity within it; then fill the bog with an acid soil mixture, and wet it until it becomes muddy and remains so.

Once you have done most of the spadework, the ferns themselves can be added. Most of the ferns for northern bogs do best in sun or light shade. One exception is the crested wood fern, which likes a well-shaded spot for its deeply arched fronds. Since these grow only 3 feet tall at maximum, you may want to plant a wood fern in the shade of an ostrich fern, which can reach a height of 8 feet when conditions are optimum.

Farther south, in Zones 8-10, gardeners with small ponds can grow the mosquito fern, a single clump of which is only an inch long at best but in the course of one summer can take over the entire surface of even a fairly large pond. It is called the mosquito fern because its rapid growth crowds the insects out of their normal breeding places, and it has been used successfully in Panama in mosquito-control programs.

BOUNDARY MARKERS

A carpet of ferns surfacing a pond or bog will hardly surprise anyone, but few think of these plants for fences. Yet they make excellent informal enclosures. Their gentle and initially inconspicuous coloration can preserve a property line without jarringly proclaiming its existence. Adjoining small yards owned by cooperative and congenial neighbors can be made to appear larger by separating them only with fern fences. The Christmas fern, a hardy evergreen that reaches a height of 2 or 3 feet and will thrive seemingly anywhere, is ideal as an unobjectionable reminder of territorial rights, and can be alternated with some of the larger ferns, such as the interrupted fern, to provide a bit of privacy.

If your property is large but irregular, a trail of informally planted ferns can be both a unifying element in the landscaping and a helpful guide to its boundaries. The trail can begin as an extremely fluid enclosure around a terrace, and briefly circle back upon itself at a point roughly halfway from the house to provide a sort of roofless gazebo. A trail can also be a subtly harmonious link between plantings of other ferns, such as a cobble or a bog.

In a fern trail, evergreen ferns should be used as extensively as possible, since deciduous ferns will leave sizable gaps until well into spring. Care is necessary in the choice of species, for some ferns grow so rampantly that they will not keep to the more or less linear requirements of a boundary marker. Their use requires a realistic, and perhaps conservative, estimate of the capabilities of your property before they are planted.

Foremost among these wayward types is the hay-scented fern, whose initial attractions include the ease with which it will grow in full sun and the pleasantly bucolic odor produced by its hirsute fronds. But it will require a judicious weeding each spring to keep it from outgrowing its space.

Bracken (*Pteridium aquilinum*), which would appear to be the answer to the unambitious gardener's prayers (it is seemingly indestructible, will grow in poor soil, is of medium size and has thick shiny fronds), is in disfavor because of its tenacity and reproductive proclivities. But for the gardener who has a lot of space to fill and very little time in which to do it, bracken has possibilities. (Part of its ill repute arises from the fact that more than 40 years ago the Department of Agriculture's *Farmer's Bulletin* classed it as a troublesome weed; another reason for its bad name is that if enough of it is eaten, it can poison horses and cattle.)

Rampart growers such as the hay-scented and bracken ferns may be undesirable along a boundary, but for another out-of-the-ordinary purpose—as a ground cover—their spreading tendencies make them valuable. They can be kept under control by pulling up or cutting back the nomadic rhizomes, which are but shallowly embedded in the soil. Disciplining a stand of ferns is nowhere near as time consuming as the constant mowings and weedings required by a lawn, and the gardener with a penchant for wild but not abandoned planting may find these complaisant ferns the solution for those areas that could present more problems than pleasures.

A FERN THAT FEEDS RICE

The mosquito fern, Azolla filiculoides, grows so fast in ponds and streams it is a nuisance. But this ordinarily troublesome weed is welcomed by rice growers. Its fronds harbor a blue-green algae that takes nitrogen from the air and converts it into a form usable as a plant nutrient. Hence, much as soybeans and clover are planted to replenish nitrogen in farm soil, mosquito ferns are cultivated in rice paddies to provide extra nutrition that increases the rice yield.

A REHABILITATED WEED

Unusual uses for unusual plants

From Quebec to Texas, the cultivated fern's ability to suggest the serenity of its natural habitats makes it a featured player—and occasionally the star—of many garden scenes. There are species to be found that will grow outdoors the year round in almost any climate, and if the plants are carefully selected and properly planted, they will flourish with only a minimum expenditure of time and effort to maintain them.

Because so many ferns are forest plants, they are often used in large masses to create man-made wildernesses, reproducing in suburban backyards the natural, unaffected charm of the native woods. This type of garden is easier to cultivate, grows better and generally is more attractive if the plants chosen are those that grow—or once grew—wild in the environment typical of the area. It may be possible to raise the ferns of British Columbia in a corner of a Southern California lot as long as the local water supply holds out, but the patch of wilderness is obviously artificial. In some regions—notably in the southeastern United States—the choice of ferns for a wilderness garden is wide and spectacular, and an idealized jungle can indeed be created (overleaf). But there are also many species native to the North that are frost-resistant. These species can be set in beds to create a woodsy refuge or scattered artfully here and there in the hospitable shade of a large tree (pages 46-47) as a simple way of bridging awkward space between a manicured terrain and the wilds beyond.

While the sprawling, naturalized display is among the most popular outdoor settings for these plants, gardeners who love ferns have found many other ways to capitalize on their distinctive beauty. One gardener keeps a number of different species potted in movable containers and shifts them about in the garden to create the effect of "plantings" of many different kinds (pages 48-49). And in the picture at right, a single fern arching over a rock terminates a pathway that leads to no particular destination but simply offers a pleasant stroll beside some flowers.

A Rocheford fern adds graceful detail to a massive boulder in the front yard of a home in Bellevue, Washington, defining the end of the wide concrete plant border.

The planned wilderness

The most admired wild gardens are those that have the appearance of being the least planned, such as the jungle garden below and the woodland garden shown on pages 46-47. Actually, both have been carefully constructed so the plants in them get the appropriate amounts of light and moisture.

The tree ferns in this central Florida garden, for example, are widely spaced to allow for the fact that they may grow a foot or more annually. They have been planted near trees to protect their slender trunks from winds and to give them the same shade they provide to the staghorn and sword ferns planted nearby.

Most of the ferns in this jungle garden are native to Florida, where the mild and constant temperatures support more than 150 indigenous species. But the owners have also brought exotic Caribbean ferns into their garden, since the man-made lagoon provides conditions that make the imports feel at home.

A lagoon adds more than charm to this jungle garden. It ensures drainage for the plants on its banks and it also helps to maintain a high humidity.

A mass of sword ferns, needing little care except daily watering, makes an attractive border planting along the path from the lagoon to the house.

Western sword ferns scattered about this woodland garden north of Seattle create a smooth transition from the backyard to the

forest beyond, while the unraked carpet of maple leaves protects the swords' roots in winter and provides humus-rich soil.

A rock-walled pool, separating the small lawn from a heavily shaded brick patio, is the setting around which ferns in pots are clustered in displays changed at the gardener's whim—from simple and airy (below, left) to heavy and lush (below, right).

Feathery foliage—all from plants in pots—clothes the bare garden pool seen in the top picture. Several species of maidenhairs line the front edge, while several taller tree ferns arch protectively above a bright cluster of camellias along the rear wall.

Every fern in the garden above has been replaced in the arrangement at right. The transformation took only a few hours, and the combination of bird's-nest and sword ferns in front with tree ferns in the rear gives the same area a more lush appearance.

Portable beds, quick changes

This garden in Encinitas, California, is portable. The owner simply removes one potted fern from the ground and replaces it with another—redecorating her garden as easily as other people move furniture around their living rooms. In the photo at left, her garden is practically bare, while the other pictures show it with different arrangements of potted ferns. The portable garden technique works as well in a New England garden with hardy ferns as it does in a Southern California or Florida garden with subtropical ferns.

There are practical as well as esthetic advantages to the portable fern garden. Insect-infested or diseased plants can easily be isolated from healthy ones. And unlike the gardeners of southern Florida who saw a rare dusting of snow destroy many of their permanent ferns in 1977, the owner of a portable fern garden has an easy way to protect his plants against meteorological vagaries— he needs only to follow the weather forecasts to know when it is time to move his ferns out of harm's way.

Indoors, an old-fashioned elegance 3

Surely the question most frequently asked of plant shop clerks is, "What do you have that doesn't need any light?" The honest answer, given in most cases, is "Nothing"; even the aspidistra, or cast-iron plant, so named because it will prosper in a Hadean gloom that would defeat most other plants, will not survive in absolute darkness. What is usually meant, however, is poor light rather than none at all, a common bane for urban and suburban plant lovers and a formidable obstacle in the case of most plants. Ferns provide the answer. Their tremulous fronds will bring a tangible suggestion of the spacious beauty that lies beyond the horizon of even the most gloomy interiors, and their continuingly modest demands will fit easily into the schedule of even the indoor gardener who is really too busy to give adequate care to most plants.

The ferns preferred for growing in the house do need some light, of course, and they respond particularly well to artificial illumination. They also should be set in a specially adapted potting mixture. But their demands for moisture are more strict. In the dry air that accompanies central heating, special measures must be taken to keep ferns flourishing. Several methods—gravel trays and double-potting among them—will supply needed moisture without getting plants so wet that their roots will rot. Occasionally, you may have to rehabilitate a dried-out plant by keeping it under plastic or in a terrarium while it recovers. But none of the techniques involved in growing ferns indoors call for unusual skill or elaborate equipment. And the result is unusual plants of unusual beauty.

The ardent outdoor gardener who is temporarily deprived by icy winters of the opportunity to engage in his hobby will find it possible to assuage some of the grief by getting to know the tropical ferns, which cannot be grown successfully outdoors in most parts of the United States and Canada.

If you are one of the multitude whose acquaintance with the

A potted Microlepia strigosa (top right) lives in house climate, but other small tropical ferns bask in high humidity—close to 95 per cent—inside a terrarium. A terrarium is also ideal for nurturing tender fern cuttings.

genus *Nephrolepis* has been limited to the ubiquitous Boston fern, *N. exaltata bostoniensis,* some fascinating discoveries await you. Descendants of the Boston fern are astonishingly varied. Many of them were produced in cultivation at the turn of the century, in what appears to have been a delayed American reaction to the fern mania of Victorian England.

The emergence of the Boston fern as a popular house plant was a lucky accident involving the sword fern *(Nephrolepis exaltata),* a widely grown house plant at the time. In 1894, in a shipment of 200 sword ferns from grower Robert Craig and Company in Philadelphia to F. C. Becker, a distributor in Cambridge, Massachusetts, one plant attracted notice for its beautiful fronds, longer and more graceful than those of the other plants.

At first, the odd fern was thought to be a new species; it was propagated and about 50,000 were marketed by Becker under the name *N. davallioides.* The validity of this designation was debated in the pages of *The Florists' Exchange,* a horticultural publication of the day, and the issue was finally settled when the Society of American Florists sent one of the new plants to the Royal Botanical Garden in England, where it was officially acknowledged a mutant offspring of the sword fern and christened *N. exaltata bostoniensis,* or the Boston fern.

MUTANTS OF THE BOSTON

Growers producing great masses of this Boston fern found that it was unstable, that is, prone to repeated mutation, its runners frequently producing offspring unlike the parent plant. Some had wavy, curly or very finely divided leaves, others had shorter, more compact fronds. One grower after another discovered and cultivated these sports and gave them extravagant names such as *elegantissima* and *superbissima.*

By 1916, when R. C. Benedict wrote a systematic and still-authoritative description of the many mutant varieties of the Boston fern, there were about 75. Many of these have been lost since, and new varieties that have appeared later often duplicate lost ones. There are now about 20 widely grown varieties. They are characterized by pinnae packed so densely that the fronds have a deeply matted appearance, making most other fern fronds look almost two dimensional in comparison. The thick tangles of verdure, accented by subtle shadings in their green coloration, make of these ferns an almost sculptural addition to a room. A further asset is their availability in a variety of sizes, from the standard Boston fern (over 3 feet tall) to the dainty Irish Lace (less than 6 inches).

Equally delightful for indoor gardening are those ferns that grow furry rhizomes and are popularly named for various animal appendages, mostly feet. To children they are an especially fascinating group, since stroking the rhizomes, while no substitute for petting a live animal, is something like rubbing a mounted rabbit's foot. Included in this group of ferns are not only the squirrel's-foot (*Davallia trichomanoides*), the rabbit's-foot (*Polypodium aureum*), the bear's-foot (*Humata tyermannii*) and the bear's-paw (*Aglaomorpha meyenianum*) but one, *Scyphularia pentaphylla*, that bears no readily discoverable common name and is hereby dubbed the monkey's-paw fern because of its black, furred rhizomes.

If you like a more ethereal look, the *Adiantum* ferns (some 200 species of maidenhairs) are unexcelled in daintiness. They are notable for salmon suffusions of young leaflets balanced precariously on wiry black stems. But a relationship with any *Adiantum* is not something to be undertaken lightly, since its need for high humidity and soil slightly drier than wet but never really dry may go on for as long as 30 years.

If you do not have the time to care for an *Adiantum,* you might want to try the Tsussima holly fern, a tough Japanese plant that will not collapse in low humidity—it makes do with less than 50 per cent—and is indifferent enough about watering to last through the winter in moderately dry soil. Its finely pierced fronds do not really resemble holly but form handsome rosettes of modest size, under a foot in length.

The plant boom has made finding a Tsussima—and most other uncommon ferns—a relatively simple matter in any city. Even a neighborhood florist or plant store is likely to have a few unusual varieties, though the asparagus fern that some of them proffer when you ask for a fern is not a fern at all but a beautiful relative of the vegetable asparagus. If your city is fortunate enough to have a botanical garden, check there in your quest for ferns. Such institutions often operate plant shops, and may have the very ferns you are seeking. If you want to assemble a tropical fern collection of any great variety, however, mail-order catalogues offer the only practical solution in many parts of the United States.

Bear in mind, however, that any ferns that you intend to keep indoors need to be carefully checked for good health even more closely than those to be planted outdoors, since a well-heated room provides a life-prolonging environment for garden pests that may attack your other house plants as well. Be sure to check both the upper and lower surfaces of all fronds to make certain they are not harboring an enemy.

Hardy ferns that are to be part of an indoor collection should generally be evergreen types, simply because many deciduous

RECLAIMING SALTY POTS

Ferns that grow sluggishly or show signs of wilting may be suffering from excess salts deposited by hard water or fertilizers. Look for whitish-gray crusty spots on the pots, a sign that such salts are present. Much of the deposit can be leached out of the soil by dunking the pot repeatedly in a bucket of water for a few minutes, letting it drain each time. If the pot is worth saving, chip off encrusted salts. If salt accumulations are a chronic problem, use plastic pots, which are less porous than clay and easier to clean of encrustations.

CHECKUP FOR NEWCOMERS

ferns in midwinter present a discouraging sight. This is true of any deciduous plant; a maple or elm bonsai can look, in the middle of the winter, like a dead twig. Tropical ferns generally do not acquire that hangdog look during the cold months.

Unlike ferns bought for an outdoor garden, those that are destined to stay indoors usually should remain in the pots they came in. For ferns are less harmed by crowded roots than other house plants; even jammed in pots with their roots protruding, they probably are not crying out for larger containers. As long as the new fronds do not appear yellow and stunted, a fern is probably best left right where it is. When a fern must be repotted it should be moved only to the next size of pot, no more than 2 inches greater in diameter than the pot it is leaving.

SATISFYING THIRST

Your most important task, though, is to give your ferns an ample water supply without drowning them. How you pot them can help you meet this stringent requirement. Set each potted fern inside a larger pot and fill the space between them with sphagnum moss. (The name is a catchall for some 300 species of mosses—not all of them from the sphagnum genus—that are not ground up but are left uncut, dried and sold in sheets.) This type of moss will absorb excess water from the inner pot and will keep its outside moist, whereas water left standing in a saucer under the pots might cause root rot. The inner pot, whether clay or plastic, must have a drainage hole. If the outer one has such a hole, plug it with a cork or florists' clay. The choice of pot material depends partly on how much attention you can pay to watering. Clay's porosity allows roots to get the free-circulating air they need, but plastic retains moisture longer. Its hard, smooth surface also discourages the accumulation of fertilizer salts, the white matter you see around the inner rim of clay pots. If you use clay pots scrub the salts off periodically. To promote drainage, put a layer of gravel or shards of broken clay pots at least an inch thick in the bottom of each pot before adding the soil mixture.

A good basic mix for most ferns consists of 1 part packaged potting soil, 1 part peat moss or leaf mold, and 1 part builder's sand. Do not use sand from an ocean beach; it is too salt-laden for ferns. Most ferns do best with a pH of 5.5 to 6.5, and this soil mix provides such a chemical balance without further amendment. The exception to this rule are those ferns native to areas where limestone is common; they do better in an alkaline soil with a pH of 7.0 to 8.0. To achieve this balance, add a tablespoon of ground limestone per gallon of mix. It is also a good idea to add 2 tablespoons of bone meal per gallon of mix; bone meal is a safe source of

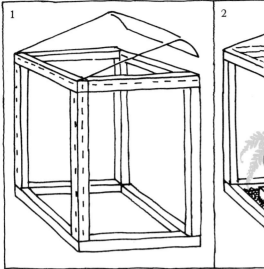 

To rejuvenate ailing ferns, build an enclosure that will keep them moist. Make a wood frame and staple plastic over the bottom and sides. Cover the top with plastic that will overlap, stapling one edge to form a lid.

Put the box in a bright spot shielded from direct sunlight and set the ferns inside on a bed of moist sphagnum moss. Prop up the pots to keep the fronds from dragging. Water thoroughly, then close the cover.

phosphorus, which helps develop strong root systems. In such a soil mixture in double pots, you should not need to water more than three times a week unless the room is very hot and dry. Lift the inner pot occasionally to check the moss. It should always be moist but never sopping wet; if it is wet, cut down to two waterings a week. If the moss feels dry, you have not been watering enough.

Moisture in the soil is not the only water that matters for ferns. They depend heavily on moisture in the air around them, measured as per cent relative humidity—you can buy an instrument called a hygrometer to indicate this figure on a dial. Most homes are too dry in winter—20 per cent or less—for ferns, and some steps must be taken to moisten the air around your plants, which require humidity above 50 per cent.

INEXPENSIVE HUMIDITY

Automatic humidifiers, made to operate on their own or in conjunction with a warm-air heating system, efficiently raise moisture levels in the air and make living space more comfortable for you as well as your plants. But you will get practically the same result for the plants at less expense by placing shallow pans of water under them. Set your pots on a layer of wet gravel in a tray or saucer. Keep the gravel uncompromisingly wet, but be certain the pots are standing on top of the stones and not in the water below, to guard against root rot. The gravel should come no higher than half an inch from the top of the rim of the saucer or tray holding it, to forestall accidental spills. As a decorative element in a room, it brings to mind austere Japanese gardens consisting of small stones in carefully raked arcs.

Most ferns also will benefit, though briefly, from an occasional misting with a water atomizer, which not only raises the humidity around their fronds, but—if applied gently but purposefully—will wash away pests. (The exceptions are ferns with finely divided foliage, such as some Boston and maidenhair ferns whose closely packed pinnae may trap moisture and turn yellow.) Many gardeners set their fern pots in a bathtub for misting, so that the excess water simply runs down the drain. If there is ample light, ferns also benefit from being kept near the tub so that when you shower the heavy mists will envelop the fern fronds instead of merely fogging the bathroom mirror.

The proper temperature is also important to a fern's well-being. Tropical ferns will generally be comfortable and perform adequately at the temperatures found in the average home, somewhere in the high 60s or low 70s during the day in winter and 10° cooler at night. The low winter temperatures required by northern ferns (40° to 50°) would make a room as comfortable as the inside of a refrigerator, and effectively relegate the indoor winter care of these species to the specialist. There is at least one interesting exception, the purple cliff brake, a northern species that will not only survive in an overheated and dry atmosphere that would defeat other ferns, but even remain evergreen throughout the winter, something it does not do outdoors in most of North America.

The removal of an occasional yellowing or browning leaf, and the tidying of the pot by cutting away a dead rhizome that no longer serves any purpose other than crowding the plant, are the only other chores you are likely to encounter routinely in the maintenance of indoor ferns.

IMAGINATIVE DISPLAYS   These procedures apply fairly generally to ferns cultivated indoors, whether you grow one or a dozen, alone or in groups, on a window sill or in big containers. There are several ways of grouping ferns in single containers that make for interesting display and, in some cases, simplify their care. The Wardian fern case, which first enabled these plants to be grown successfully indoors, is once again immensely popular, as are hanging baskets. And an enjoyable alternative to a collection of random-sized clay pots, which are handsome enough in any room but require attention in watering (and often result, despite one's best efforts, in a collection of rust-colored rings and flaky patches on the sills and other surfaces that support them), is the creation of an indoor fern bed or rock garden. Almost any watertight container at least 5 inches deep will serve as a foundation for such a planting. A metal or plastic window box is suitable, as is even a deep roasting pan that has outlived its usefulness in the kitchen.

At the bottom of the future bed, place a 1-inch layer of gravel to absorb excess moisture. Above the gravel place as deep a layer of soil as can be accommodated while still allowing a rim an inch deep around the top of the container. The basic fern soil mix described on page 54 should be used. Rake the soil so that it is slightly higher at the rear than in the front; this will give you some slight additional soil drainage and will provide a more interesting topography for the bed as well.

Though ferns for the indoor bed need not be especially low growing, there will not be enough space for very many of them, and the largest should, of course, be placed at the back. Ideally, the ferns for the indoor bed should be such slow growers as the medium-sized (about 2 feet, on the average) climbing bird's-nest fern, which does not climb at all but actually creeps or clumps. It is not related to another fern of similar name that is also a good choice for a bed, the far better known nonclimbing bird's-nest fern, which, while not as slow growing, provides striking rosettes composed of what look like elongated green shoehorns. The dwarf Boston fern is another slow grower, and it can bring to the limited area of the bed a compact summation of the qualities that have made its larger counterparts so spectacularly popular.

The bed can be interestingly varied by introducing touches of color in the form of rosy maidenhair or the hammock fern. Both kinds produce fronds that are delicately reddish in their young stages. (It is almost impossible to find color that is in any way garish on a fern, even when that color is red.) These are both tropical ferns that stay well under a foot in height, so they can remain as permanent accents in the fern bed.

An indoor bed can be temporarily converted into a miniature greenhouse by sticking short garden stakes into the corners and using them as supports for a roof and sides of plastic or similar materials. Something as flimsy as the garment bag that protects your clothes on their way back from the dry cleaner's is perfectly adequate, and it can be frequently replaced at no cost above that of your cleaning bills. Moisture will be conserved for long periods within this makeshift shelter, and ferns inside it can be noticeably revitalized. Ferns not normally part of the bed, such as those in pots, can be benefited by placing them temporarily inside this structure, between other ferns if there is space, or in a similar temporary greenhouse of their own *(page 55)*.

While the fern bed permits you to mass these plants in an expansive display, the fern case provides an attention-catching focal point of their lacy beauty. A totally enclosed collection of ferns is no less beautiful today than it was over a hundred years ago when Dr. Ward was greening both the stately and the humble homes of England with his popular fern cases. Esthetic and inexpensive housing for a fern collection is readily available now in the aquarium tank that is constructed without metal corners, and this enables the ferns to be seen as though they were growing out of doors. You can also make a fern case out of a demijohn stripped of its straw basket, or any other container that is transparent and has an opening large enough to put plants through. Soil and gravel can be poured into narrow-necked vessels by using a funnel or a rolled-up newspaper; glassware with a neck too narrow to put your hand through can be planted by pushing plants freed of their soil through the opening and setting them into the soil mix with long tongs.

A FERN CASE LANDSCAPE   The bottom of the fern case is prepared in the same manner as the fern bed—layers of gravel and soil—except that crushed charcoal is mixed with the gravel, to absorb impurities that cannot escape the small enclosed space that offers neither drainage nor air circulation. The fern case will be far more dramatic if you build several soil levels before adding the plants; you might even want to construct a miniature fern cobble within the confines of your four glass walls, or recreate a hilly scene you are familiar with. A plunging gorge can be created by simply placing two pieces of rock so that there is an inch or two of space between them, and embedding them so that there are two resulting planting levels, one at the base of the rocks and one behind and above them. You can send an imitation cataract rampaging down the gorge by trickling some ordinary gravel down the slope between the rocks.

Plant your fern case with varieties that are small—and are likely to remain so. Some descendants of the Boston fern are good choices. Dwarf Fluffy Ruffles is one that is not only easily located in commercial plant stores but will dependably accommodate itself to the requirements of fern cases, rarely reaching a height of more than 8 inches, and usually less. It is also exceedingly comely, since its tiny fronds are so intensely ruffled that they appear to be made of something less substantial than plant tissue. It has dozens of small relatives, not all as easily available as it is, but many worth a search. *Nephrolepis cordifolia compacta* is dependably small—less than 9 inches—and has spearlike fronds of more substantial texture. Plant them on the different levels that you have created in your fern case, and accentuate their green beauty with miniature ferns that provide daubs of color, such as the Victorian brake (striped with white) and the rosy maidenhair (pink when young).

Ferns are not the only things that will grow in a fern case, which becomes known as a terrarium when other plants are introduced into it. These newcomers need only share the tropical fern's proclivity for growing at room temperatures and in shaded light to make ideal companions in the tropical terrarium. Most of the small plants used in terrariums are grown primarily for their foliage, which can at times be spectacular—the pink polka dot, whose otherwise ordinary green leaves look as though they had been spattered with rosy blobs from the brush of a particularly careless house painter, comes immediately to mind. But there are several different kinds of plants grown mainly for their flowers, such as miniature sinningias and begonias.

When your fern case is planted, fit it with a snug cover especially cut for it. Sealed in this way, it does not need watering, using and re-using the supply it already has. It is theoretically possible for the moisture in a well-sealed terrarium to be recirculated indefinitely. Dr. Ward wrote of one which had "received no fresh water for eighteen years" and went on to state that "it would

RECIRCULATING WATER

A SELF-WATERING CASE

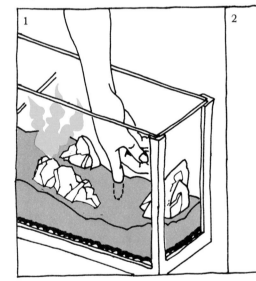 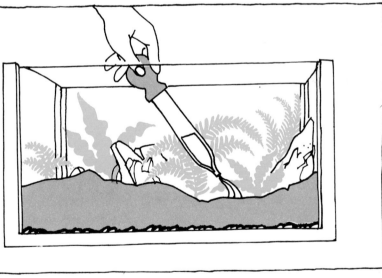

For a fern case that recycles moisture, use an aquarium tank containing 1 inch of gravel mixed with charcoal. Add a thin layer of sphagnum moss, then 2 inches of potting mix. Poke holes with your finger to plant tiny ferns.

Use a bulb baster to provide moisture, dampening the soil while keeping the fronds dry so that they are less vulnerable to fungus disease. Place a sheet of glass over the case; if heavy droplets of moisture condense on it overnight, wipe them off and leave the lid ajar the next night to reduce the humidity. Repeat until only a fine mist condenses on glass near the soil, then leave the glass cover on. Do not add more water until misting stops.

be possible to fill a case with palms and ferns and that it would not require water for fifty or a hundred years." Dr. Ward's optimism is shared by few modern fern growers, who watch the "steam" that clouds a fern case's glass to tell whether or not it needs watering. So long as this vapor appears on the glass, recycling of water is taking place within the terrarium.

In most cases, such condensation will disappear long before 18 months, to say nothing of 18 years, have elapsed. When the inner surface of the glass appears totally dry, remove the cover and give the terrarium a heavy watering. But be careful not to flood it, since there is no place for the surplus water to run off to, and overwatering increases the danger of fungus or mold, almost the only ills by which closed cases are beset. The cover also should be removed occasionally to allow some fresh air to circulate throughout the case, as a retardant to the formation of fungus, and all dead fronds or leaves should be removed as soon as they are detected, since it is upon them that mold usually begins. Living tissue that has been attacked should be cut away promptly. A fungicide can be applied if all else fails; however, it usually is not necessary if a terrarium is kept under close surveillance so problems can be detected early and good sanitation is maintained.

INDOOR ROCK GARDENS   Like the fern case, a display of rocks and ferns can make a spectacular point of interest indoors. Ferns and rocks are so harmonious a combination of natural materials out of doors, in the cobble or the rock garden, that miniature plantings of them are almost equally popular indoors. A good material for this purpose is lava or volcanic rock, also known as feather rock or pumice stone, available at some variety and plant stores. You generally find it there already bored with holes into which plants are to be set. But if you can, pick up a large undrilled chunk of the material at a stoneyard, for then you can drill bigger holes into it to make room for a generous amount of soil for your ferns. Use a masonry bit in an electric drill or a hammer and chisel—the stone cuts easily—but wear gloves, safety goggles and a breathing mask while performing this work, since the abrasive dust is dangerous. If you are lucky enough to find a handsomely contoured rock while on a stroll in the country, or even to discover a possibility-rich chunk of masonry or brick while passing a rubble-strewn city demolition site, you may be spared the necessity of drilling out your own planting vessels. (In England, the wall rue is often grown in an upended brick.) The result of your labor will be a planter that will give the suggestion of some of the wilder outcroppings of nature—a rocky crag in the Highlands of Scotland, perhaps, or the stalagmite-laden floor of a

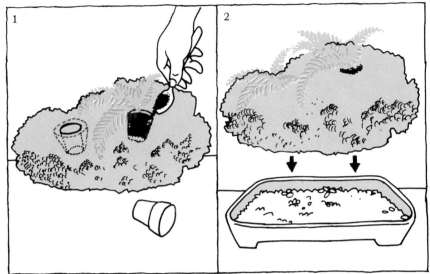

To plant small ferns such as hacksaw in lava rock—sold predrilled with holes for this purpose—put a bit of gravel in each hole, then fill with potting soil. To enlarge a hole (dotted lines, left) use a chisel; wear goggles.

Set the planted rock in a low bonsai dish atop a 1-inch layer of pebbles, and put the dish in filtered sunlight. Water the ferns daily and, for high humidity, keep the water level in the dish above the top of the pebbles.

cave—and will provide an easily maintained as well as attractive home for your small ferns.

To provide some drainage, place a very thin layer of gravel or sand at the bottom of the completed hole, perhaps half an inch (there will not be room for much more in even a large rock). Fill the opening with the soil mixture prescribed for pots. Any small fern suited to pots can be planted. But if the temperature in your home is lower than that of most, the wall rue, at 3 inches the smallest of the spleenworts and one of the smallest of all ferns, can be counted on to enhance your rock with its cuneiform leaves all year long. The maidenhair spleenwort will provide a seasonal rosette of tiny button-bedecked fronds that attain twice the size of the wall rue at best, and will be a pleasingly proportioned foil for it. Both these plants need an alkaline soil, pH 7.5 to 8.5.

If you have a very large rock, with many openings, a most effective accent for the ferns is to cap one or two of the apertures with a simple patch of moss (cut away as much of the soil beneath it as you can before setting it in place) or a clump of baby's tears, which looks like a knot of tiny clovers and spreads quickly. So do the tropical species of *Selaginella,* a 600-strong genus of plants, some similar to true ferns in appearance. The spreading variety *S. kraussiana aurea* is a particularly handsome miniature trailing plant

HANGING SCULPTURES

that will send its delicate golden tips clambering fearlessly over the rough face of any rock.

Once planted, your miniature Gibraltar should be thoroughly watered and kept on a bed of wet gravel, which can be confined temporarily in something as utilitarian as the plastic tray from a supermarket lamb chop, if need be. For a truly worthy enhancement of the rock, however, it is worth investing in an unglazed ceramic tray of the waterproof sort made expressly to be placed under bonsai pots. The undersides of these trays have multiple ridges to support the pressure of heavy weights upon them and will not crack under the weight of heavy rocks; their dull brown finish suggests both the appearance and the solidity of the earth itself, and they form perfect pedestals for objects dedicated to the celebration of nature.

To contrast with the earth-bound look of most of your ferns, or simply because you have run out of surfaces upon which to keep them, you may wish to take to the air and hang some epiphytes dramatically on bark or in openwork baskets. If your staghorn from the garden center did not arrive trussed to a slab of bark or half of a dried coconut husk and you wish to mount it, place a wet mixture of equal parts of sphagnum moss and chopped osmunda fiber between the round shield frond and a piece of rough bark. A chunk of cork bark is ideal and supplies a dramatically textured background. Bind fern to support with a length of nylon string—wire may injure or poison the plant.

The various "footed" ferns, such as rabbit's-foot and its cohorts, can be grown in especially manufactured wire baskets that look very much like those used for egg storage in French kitchens. Other suitable carriers for such furry rhizomes are redwood slat baskets. The interior of the basket should be filled with uncut moss, dried or not, and filled with the airiest soil mixture that can be concocted—equal parts of shredded bark, peat moss and sand, for example—and the fern planted as shallowly as can be, with the alluringly fuzzy rhizomes exposed as fully as possible.

Victorians amused themselves by hanging from their ceilings ferns trained to the shapes of anything from simple spheres to life-like monkeys. This was accomplished through the use of prepared wire forms that were sold in stores and were apparently routine plant accessories at the time. A modern version can easily be made with chicken wire. The interior of the frame is packed with sphagnum moss and the fern roots are bound to the wire so that they root in the moss. The favorite fern for this hobby in Victorian times was the scaly hare's-foot, whose generously branching rhizomes become particularly flexible when they are wet down. This fern is deciduous, but its rhizomes are thickly encrusted with reddish-brown scales throughout the year, and even in its dormancy the fern sculpture evidently was attractive enough to be left hanging in some presumably cold corner of the parlor.

Hanging ferns, whether in baskets or on bark, have to be taken down for occasional waterings. Epiphytes should be set under a faucet or dunked in a bucket whenever their growing medium feels dry to the touch. Ferns on high will also have to be misted more frequently than those down below, since they dry faster in their more exposed position and will be subjected to higher temperatures because of the rising of warm air in the room.

Hanging containers are particularly useful in placing ferns so that they get the illumination they need. In many cases, it is easier to hang a plant near a window than to find space there to set a pot. In addition, the simple pulley device that is intended to raise and lower the container so you can tend to its plant also serves the purpose of enabling you to position the plant high or low for proper illumination. But some homes are so shrouded in darkness all day long that neither at floor nor ceiling level is there sufficient light to support a fern. In city apartments, it is by no means uncommon to need to turn on a lamp for reading at midday, and even in a suburban home some rooms may be almost totally screened from the sun by trees or neighboring houses. For such situations, artificial illumination is necessary and, in the case of ferns, fairly simple.

Ferns will thrive on a mere 200 to 600 foot-candles of light, a need easily met by hanging 1 foot above them an ordinary fluorescent fixture fitted with two cool-white 40-watt tubes. Keep them on for 12 hours a day, which seems to be the happiest light duration for ferns. These lamps will light the ferns for some 9,000 hours; though they last longer, they should be retired before they start to dim. At 12 hours a day, this is a bit more than two years.

SUPPLEMENTAL LIGHT

This simple scheme will illuminate an area 4 feet long (the length of the fluorescent tubes) and 2 feet wide (the width of the swath usably lit). It will provide light that, though not sufficient to flower geraniums, is more than adequate to elicit the best efforts from ferns as diverse as the southern maidenhair, which luxuriates in low light, and the sword fern, which will, if need be, stand up to the full force of the sun's rays.

For those who must continue to dwell in dark places, ferns grown under artificial lights provide a pleasure that might have been despaired of. It is a pleasure easily attained, and it is better, after all, to light a fluorescent tube than to curse the darkness.

Versatility of the potted fern

If potted fern suggests only Boston fern, take a look at the pictures opposite and on the following pages. There are hundreds of varieties of ferns for indoor pots. Some grow like moss on the surface of water; others billow or trail; their leaflets can be asymmetrical or even nonexistent. Still others, instead of being uniformly green, are impregnated or overlaid with yellow, red or white.

Many of the shapes, textures and colors of these plants are actually survival mechanisms that for 350 million years have enabled them to compete successfully for food, moisture and living space in the dense tangle of the jungle and forest growth that is their native habitat. The unsegmented fronds of the bird's-nest fern form a nest shape to hold nutrient-rich humus. The staghorn fern stores water in the round, spongelike basal leaf that clings to tree trunks in the wild. And the fine gold dust on the undersides of the goldback fern's leaves is also a water-holding device.

But evolutionary adaptations do not account for all the variations among ferns. In England in the late 19th Century, human beings picked up where nature left off. The darlings of the Victorians were the mutant ferns, those with leaf shapes or growth patterns that differed from those of their parent plants. These curiosities were sought and bred in England to achieve plants such as the crested hart's-tongue fern, with its elaborately scalloped foliage, and in America to develop the numerous versions of the ornamental Boston fern that graced every fashionable parlor of the day. When the early fern craze waned, some cultivated varieties were lost, but renewed interest has once again broadened the selection.

Pictured opposite is part of the fern collection of Barbara McMartin, whose more than 100 plants occupy almost every room of her suburban New York home. Situated on a rocky ledge in a ravine 55 feet above a river, the house is a nearly perfect setting for ferns. In summer the air is humid, and huge hemlocks provide the filtered sunlight of a forest setting. In fact, the house, once an inn, was the site where the first Tarzan movie was filmed.

Sunlight thinned by hemlock trees falls across a luxuriant array of Boston, bird's-nest, rabbit's-foot and goldback ferns decorating Barbara McMartin's living room.

An array of shapes

In general appearance, ferns range from the flamboyant, massive staghorn to the demure mosquito fern floating on the surface of a saucerful of water. They may grow in the bold basket shape of the bird's-nest fern, which forms a capacious container for the emerging fiddleheads at its base, or in the airy, linear design of the delicate anemia with its stalks, fronds and beadlike reproductive organs set apart at three different levels. In some, the most striking visual detail is an oddity, like the distinctive furry roots of the squirrel's-foot fern, which loop and coil over the edge of the container and snake among the diaphanous foliage.

A spongy base, which looks rather like a suction cup, anchors a staghorn fern to a vertical support.

Suggesting a modern piece of wire sculpture, anemia's spore-bearing parts rise far above the leaflets.

The fan-shaped, lacy fronds of the squirrel's-foot fern are encircled by the furry curls and loops of its exposed rhizomes.

A mosquito fern spreads over the water in a mat so dense that it is said to discourage mosquitoes from breeding.

The bird's-nest fern's radiating, unfernlike, unsegmented leaves account for its basket shape.

Fronds of many configurations

The leaves, or fronds, of ferns can be flat or undulating, leathery slick or powdery, smooth-edged or divided into hundreds of tiny leaflets. Even within a single genus, two related ferns may bear little outward resemblance to each other. Between the deeply ruffled fronds of the bird's-nest fern at far right and the gently rippling fronds of the bird's-nest fern on the preceding page there is only a common habit of growth to relate them. And in the deeply cut and crimped contours of the crested hart's-tongue fern at right below there is scarcely a trace of the smooth tongue-shaped leaf of the parent plant that gave this species its name.

Billowing sprays of maidenhair fern subdivide into fan-shaped leaflets that overlap and silhouette each other.

Fronds with asymmetrical, spiky edges and crested tips distinguish this Cretan brake fern from other varieties of the species.

Cascading masses of fronds on a variety of Boston fern are so finely cut that the plant appears translucent in the sun.

The shirred fronds of a ruffled bird's-nest fern, nicknamed the lasagna plant, end in scrolled tips.

Veins and spore clusters form visible patterns on the convoluted fronds of a crested hart's-tongue fern.

69

An unexpected bonus of color

Most amazing of all the discoveries people make about ferns is that they are not always green. White or shades of red or yellow may color all or part of a plant during its life. Though the mature fronds of the hacksaw fern are green, the young fronds are a clear, deep red; the fronds of the goldback fern are coated with a fine yellow powder, but only on the undersides. Colors may also differ greatly among closely related ferns, dramatically altering their characters. The sturdy-looking green-and-white maidenhair fern on the opposite page, for example, is actually a member of the same species as the delicate rose-colored maidenhair fern on page 73.

The red in a hacksaw fern's young fronds comes from a pigment visible in the plant before it produces the chlorophyll that eventually turns the fronds green.

A colorful moisture-trapping powder coats the undersides of the fronds of a goldback fern.

White stripes and splotches on a variegated maidenhair fern result from a lack of chlorophyll.

Even as unfurling fiddleheads, the fronds of a goldback fern are coated on one side with a distinctive bright yellow, waxy powder.

The young frond of a hacksaw fern, still flushed with red, stands out from the green of the mature fronds.

A rose-tinted maidenhair has translucent stalks and leaflets so fragile they may break if heavily misted.

The tricky art of propagating seedless plants 4

In today's fast-paced world, there is a special pleasure in propagating your own ferns. It may take months for the first young ferns grown from spores to appear on the soil, but when they do, you will have the satisfaction of having created something with your own hands instead of rushing out to buy it.

Of course, saving money is an important factor in deciding to propagate your own ferns, given the fluctuating—usually higher—prices for commercially grown ferns. And if patience is one of your virtues, you can grow enough from spores in two years (the average time it will take before they are ready for the outdoor bed) to cover your property with nothing but ferns.

Possibly the greatest advantage of home propagation is that it enables you to expand your collection in the face of boundaries imposed by geography. Unusual tropical ferns may be unavailable where you live, but a friend may have a precious fern that could be divided—without harm to the plant and with great benefit to you. The staghorn fern, for example, will sometimes produce a bud that, when it has swelled to a breadth of several inches, can be cut away from the parent and mounted on a slab of bark or planted in an airy soil mixture (page 76). If you slice beneath and around the base shield with a sharp knife and replant this portion, the part of the parent plant that clings to it will benefit the new plant and will not be missed by the parent.

Division, as is used on staghorns, provides the easiest and fastest way to propagate ferns. What you divide depends on the fern—even a part of a frond will do for a few species, and others drop off little sections that reproduce. But most ferns are duplicated by dividing a cluster of crowns, the thickened vertical stems aboveground, or one of the rhizomes, the thickened horizontal stems that run just beneath the soil or on its surface.

The simplest way to propagate ferns that have a number of

A high-speed camera captures a maidenhair fern reproducing—the fine dust is ripe spores, ejected from spherical yellow spore sacs, which burst as they dry out. The plumper dots are clusters of spores.

wandering rhizomes (the furry-footed ones, for example) is to encourage them to grow over the rims of their pots during spring and summer and into another container conveniently placed cheek by jowl with their own *(page 77)*. Use the basic soil mixture for container-grown ferns—equal parts of packaged potting soil, peat moss or leaf mold, and builder's sand, plus 2 tablespoons of bone meal per gallon of mix. New roots will eventually be sunk into the soil of the second pot as the rhizome makes itself at home there. It can be helped to adjust to its new position by fastening it to the soil with a hairpin or bent paper clip until it develops new roots that are able to stabilize it. The addition of a surface layer of uncut sphagnum moss will help to assure the sustained moisture that the roots require. When the new roots have attained some length, cut the rhizome from the parent fern with a sharp, clean knife at the point toward the rim of the second container just behind where the new root formation has taken place.

MULTIPLYING BY DIVISION

Rhizomes can also be divided by simply cutting them from the parent fern and planting them. New plants will be established faster and more successfully if the rhizome pieces are already rooted. But rooted or without roots, plant them at the same depth as they were previously growing. The cut should be made at what looks like a logical place—a narrow neck in the rhizome or a patch

MOUNTING A BABY STAGHORN

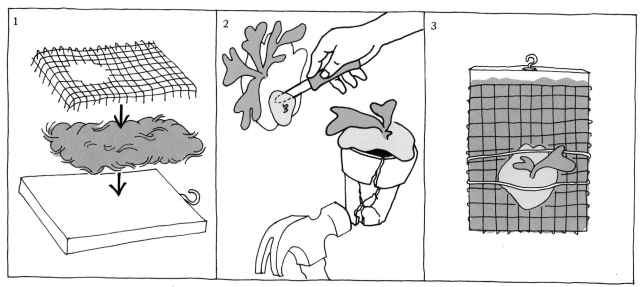

Prepare a mount for a baby staghorn by covering a 10-by-12-inch board with 2 inches of moist sphagnum moss and chopped osmunda fiber. Staple over this medium ½-inch-mesh screening with a 3-inch hole cut below center.

Obtain the baby staghorn by cutting a bud and its shield frond from the mother fern, including an inch of back material. If the baby fern is already potted, break the pot to avoid damaging the plant.

Press the bud into the medium so that the shield frond is centered over the hole and the smaller frond points upward. Tie the shield in place with nylon string. Dip board and plant in water, then drain before hanging.

devoid of growth. Broken or discolored fronds attached to the rhizome should be cut all the way back, and even some of the healthy ones cut back by half to lessen the load on the severed rhizome, which must supply them with water and nourishment. However, it is necessary to leave at least one third of the fronds to produce needed chlorophyll.

The cut ends of newly divided rhizomes should be dusted with fungicide before they are planted. They will also require an even level of soil moisture, damp but not soggy. Avoid fluctuations between dry and wet conditions.

Ferns that form crowns are more difficult to divide than those that spread by means of wandering rhizomes. But such division is possible if the plant has formed at least two crowns or if the original crown has developed offshoots. If a single crown is divided, you are likely to kill both the fern and the division. The best times to divide crown-forming ferns are early spring and fall. If the plant is not too old and the crown has not become too tough, it should be possible to break off the new crown or offshoot with your hand, somewhat as you might break a clove of garlic off a clump. If the crown does not yield to such a gentle approach, use a sharp knife to cut it off. A screwdriver or chisel can also be inserted at the desired break-off point and pressed downward between the crowns until

TWO WAYS TO PROPAGATE FROM CREEPING RHIZOMES

A fern with rhizomes that creep along the soil surface can be multiplied from cuttings of the rhizomes. In the method illustrated above, a rhizome is encouraged to sprout roots in a second pot containing ½ inch of gravel plus a mixture of potting soil and peat moss. Position the pots so a young rhizome rests on soil in the second pot, kept moist as roots form. Sever the rooted rhizome near the pot rim and dust the cut ends with fungicide.

A rhizome also can be severed first and then rooted if it is kept from drying out. Bury the cut end in soil mix, anchoring the tip with bent wire. Water, trim fronds in half, then put the pot in a clear plastic bag.

the new crown or offshoot snaps off. Be careful not to damage the growing tip of either new or old fern; it is from those buds that all new growth will develop.

Plant the newly separated crowns immediately in their new locations to about the depth at which they formerly grew, being careful not to cover the growing tips with soil. The soil should be the same mixture that supports the parent ferns, but it is helpful to mix it with some water-retentive peat moss or leaf mold. Keep the soil moist but not soggy until the plant has become well established—at least a month.

FROND-TIP INFANTS Some familiar ferns have the endearing ability to present you with new plants already growing on their fronds, ready for the taking if you simply separate them and see them off to a good start.

With species that bear new plants at the tips of their mature fronds such as the walking fern, the end of a frond nurturing a bud can be weighted down with soil or a pebble so the plantlet is encouraged to root. A walking fern is difficult to establish, taking anywhere from two to six months for the plantlet to become well rooted, depending on whether the climate is mild or severe. To test how well such a plantlet is rooted, tug gently on it. Firm resistance means a good root system has been established. When the plantlet has developed roots, it can be separated from the parent and planted. It needs shade and high humidity until it is well established in its new location.

Another, somewhat different cooperative fern is *Polystichum setiferum,* or soft shield fern, which presents its young neatly lined up in rows on its fronds. You can cut the portion of a frond bearing these plantlets into small sections and plant them shallowly. Cover the pot with a tent of plastic film until the plantlets have rooted.

Tropical ferns that will produce similar buds to be clipped from their fronds and planted the same way include two aspleniums, *A. bulbiferum* and *A. viviparum,* as well as the trailing maidenhair, which behaves somewhat as does the walking fern and will benefit from the second-pot method of bud nurturing.

BEARERS OF BULBILS A somewhat different reproductive method of ferns resembles the planting of seeds. It can be used only on ferns that have bulbils, which are produced most interestingly of all by the bladder ferns, a genus of some 20 ethereal species (indeed, one species, *Cystopteris bulbifera,* is so insubstantial physically that it must sometimes be helped to rise by the construction of a temporary scaffolding of twigs piled around its base). The bulbils look rather like enormously inflated spores, and will fall to the ground at maturity and produce young ferns.

To separate a plantlet that sprouts from the leaflet of a frond, cut it off when it has grown ¾ inch tall. You can cut the entire plantlet-bearing frond, a portion of it (red marks) or ½ inch of the leaflet as indicated in the inset.

To establish a plantlet, pin it in moist, sterile soil in a 2-inch pot; keep the pot on wet gravel in a covered plastic box until the plantlet roots. To establish many plantlets, pin the whole frond in a box on soil over gravel.

The bulbils can be gathered like berries and planted in the standard fern soil mixture. They are, of course, far easier to handle than powder-like spores, and can be set into the soil as nonchalantly as flower and vegetable seeds. Though sowing is somewhat easier than it is with spores, the wait for a mature result is, alas, equally long, and patience will be necessary for as much as two years before a sizable fern results from this effort.

The palm, if one may be awarded to a fern for perseverance in reproducing itself even after all hope would appear to be gone, must surely be awarded to a bulbil-producing fern, the hart's-tongue, which pushes itself to propagatory efforts unknown to other ferns. Even if a frond has withered, the petiole, or lowest portion of the leaf stalk, so long as it is green, can be detached, then planted in a covered container and kept in bright indirect light at 70° to 75°. In a month or so, the stem portion will be covered with minute bulbils, which may then be removed and planted as independently of the parent as are the bulbils of other ferns.

Propagating ferns from divisions is simple and fast, and it yields new plants identical to their parents, so you always know what you are getting. But it does not increase your stock as much as using nature's own method of growing from spores—large multiplication may be desirable if you intend to create a sizable bed or

NATURAL REPRODUCTION

use ferns as a ground cover. And spore propagation, being sexual, introduces genetic variety; your new plants will resemble their parents but generally will not be exact duplicates. The process of using spores from your ferns is very much the same as using seeds of other types of plants.

Spores that are ready to propagate announce their intentions unmistakably in the appearance of their cases, or sporangia, which generally take on a brown color as they mature. Individual sporangia, visible with a magnifying glass, look as though they are ready to burst, while those that have already burst will look frayed, or at least depleted, with cracked husks halfheartedly clinging to the underside of the fronds.

THE SPORE HARVEST

Cut away only a portion of a frond that is rich in sporangia. You may have to pick the entire frond of a small fern such as the northern maidenhair, but you certainly will not need all the spores produced by the frond of a large fern. Place the frond on a sheet of paper. The spores will begin to emerge from their coverings almost immediately, and the exodus from the sporangia will be completed in only a few days. The usable spores will look like a fine powder when they are spread on the paper; the color of the spores themselves, unlike the color of the sporangia, which serves as a guide to the ripeness of its contents, indicates nothing, and may cover a wide range from black for some *Dryopteris* species to green for the *Osmunda* ferns. Fold and tilt the paper *(page 85)* and tap it gently to separate the spores from the chaff.

(If you live in an area so bereft of ferns that it is difficult to obtain spores, you may want to join an organization such as The

(continued on page 84)

The Bostons: a line of freaks

The plant that commercial grower John Ekstrand is examining at right is a freak—one of many that make up the widely popular group of Boston ferns. All are mutations, chance aberrant offspring of a single plant first noticed in 1894 in a shipment of 200 sword ferns from Philadelphia to Boston. This original mutant, similar in appearance to the one pictured, had broader, more graceful fronds than sword ferns and proved to be the founder of a whole line of attractive freaks—its runners and those of its descendants frequently produced other mutants.

The mutation-prone Boston ferns quickly surpassed the ancestral sword fern in popularity and began to be mass-produced in commercial greenhouses, where growers culled plants for aberrant specimens with such desirable features as finely divided leaves, compact growth or deeply curled leaflets. By 1920 about 75 varieties were known, but today only about 20 are widely cultivated, among the best-liked being the eight on the following pages, photographed in Ekstrand's California greenhouse.

Fern specialist John Ekstrand examines a plant like the ancestral Boston fern, progenitor of scores of different varieties.

The Boston fern named Fluffy Ruffles has crisp, curly edges.

Trevillian resembles Fluffy Ruffles but has softer fronds.

Rooseveltii plumosa has undulating leaflets, but otherwise is like the original Boston fern pictured on the preceding page.

Young leaflets of Whitman are typically widely spaced.

The aptly named Irish Lace has delicately edged foliage.

Spiky new fronds contrast with Norwood's plumy mass.

Some of Splendida's fronds end in cascading clumps.

Wagner's elaborate fronds are twisted as well as ruffled.

American Fern Society and participate in its spore exchange, as several thousand fern fanciers do each year.)

Since the germination rate of ferns is no closer to 100 per cent than that of the seeds of other plants and you really have no idea of what success to expect, plant as many as you can. Use several containers that can be filled to a depth of about an inch—clear plastic boxes, refrigerator storage containers or ordinary flowerpots are fine. Scrub them with detergent and a solution of 1 part bleach to 9 parts of water, then rinse thoroughly, since any contamination may harm the spores.

Cover the bottom of each container with a layer of gravel or vermiculite for drainage. Wet it thoroughly, then prepare the basic soil mix for ferns and put it through a sieve so every possible obstacle that might get in the way of a struggling sprout is removed. Pour boiling water through this soil mix several times. When the mix has cooled and drained, fill the container with about an inch of moist (not soggy) mix.

Gently tap the folded paper to distribute the spores as evenly as possible on the surface of the soil mix. Then cover the container with a sheet of clear plastic; if it has been sufficiently watered at the outset, the container will recycle moisture like a terrarium and probably require not more than an occasional misting. When you must, however, use sterile water—boiled for several minutes, then allowed to cool to room temperature. Spores planted in flowerpots can be watered by setting the pots in saucers of sterile water; when the surface of the soil becomes damp, remove the pots from the water and let them drain.

NEW LIFE BEGINS   Keep the container in bright north-window light—but never direct sunlight—at a temperature of 68° to 86°. It will be a week or so before the first microscopic stirrings occur and about three weeks before a green cast can be seen if the spores were densely sown. In a couple of months, the sexual plants, or prothallia, all of a quarter of an inch long, become visible. (Not all ferns appear this quickly; the staghorn fern, for example, can take as long as a year to sprout anything at all from spores.)

When the green fuzz on the surface of the germination vessel begins to resemble a newly sprouted patch of lawn planted in clover, it is time to thin the growth, or transplant some of it, to avoid crowding and spindly growth. Move ¼-inch clumps, setting them about ½ inch apart. At this stage it is crucial for moisture to be present on the surface of the sprouts, for it is now that the sperm are making their attempts to reach the eggs at the other ends of the tiny prothallium leaves, and if the new foliage is not kept glisten-

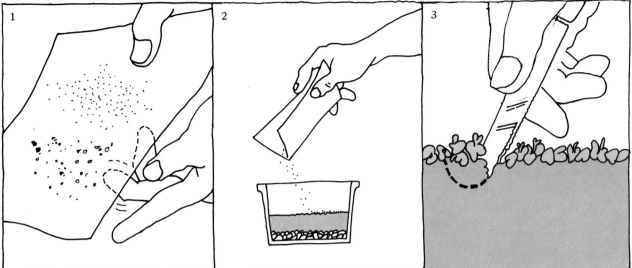

To winnow spore casings from spores, place them on a sheet of paper after they have been separated from fronds and dried. Tilt and tap the paper to dislodge bits of casing and leave the smaller spores behind.

Sow the spores in a clean glass bowl that has been lined with ½ inch of gravel and topped with an inch of pasteurized soil dampened with sterile water. Cover with plastic wrap and place in a bright, sunless spot.

When young ferns have developed from the prothallia (page 19) and are about an inch tall, dig ¼-inch clumps with the tip of a knife and pot the clusters of plants. Pot individually when ferns are 2 to 3 inches tall.

ingly wet these strivings will be in vain. Mist frequently to make sure the plants stay wet.

Some nine months after sowing the spores, you will have identifiable young ferns, or sporophytes, poking their way up from the clumps of prothallia below them. Exact times vary with species. The northern maidenhair will make you wait only six months for it to produce its young from spores, while the staghorn takes two to three years to achieve the same result.

When the young ferns are fingerlings an inch or so in height they should be thinned again and transplanted. The plastic covering of the germinating pan should be removed at this time, and fish-emulsion fertilizer diluted to half the strength recommended on the label should be applied monthly.

The chief responsibility facing the propagator at this stage of development, other than that of maintaining adequate moisture for the new fern crop, is to be watchful for signs of a fungus invasion. If such symptoms are present, discard not only the plants that have been attacked but also those nearby, and spray the container thoroughly with half-strength fungicide. It is better to give up a few young plants rather than to try to save them, since you should have many healthy ones left.

When the young ferns have reached 2 to 3 inches in height,

CONTROLLING FUNGUS

about a year later, they can be planted individually in small, sterilized pots, in fresh soil identical to the mixture that was used in germinating them. The fertilized prothallia will have obligingly removed themselves from the scene meanwhile. From this point on, the care of the new young ferns is just about what it is for those that are mature. Ferns whose final destination is the outdoors should be exposed to its rigors gradually by being stationed temporarily in such sheltered locations as sun porches and areaways after they are two years old.

THE LURE OF HYBRIDIZING   Who can blame the newly successful propagator, heady with achievement at having grown ferns from spores, for envisioning himself a latter-day Luther Burbank, ready to bestow upon a waiting world a crossbreed that will startle every observer with its distinctions? Unfortunately, the world is not ready to beat a path to the door of the person who hybridizes a better fern. For one thing, there are still too many problems connected with propagating hybrids after they have been developed, since they do not reproduce dependably, even if they are not entirely sterile, as most are. Furthermore, since it is unlikely that hybridization will produce a fern that looks or acts radically different from its parents—as a rule ferns that are very different from each other cannot even produce hybrids—there is little incentive to invest great amounts of money or time in crossbreeding.

However, the home hybridizer can have an interesting and even exciting time of it, and perhaps even come up with something that will make the professionals take notice. Kathryn Boydston of Niles, Michigan, began growing ferns from spores in 1958. A few years later she happened to sow spores of walking ferns and hart's-tongue ferns together in the same glass dish, "making the sort of mistake any amateur might make," she says. Among the hundreds of offspring was one hybrid, halfway between the two ferns in size, shape and vein pattern. Its form proved to be so unusual that its fronds have since been added to the taxonomic collections at the University of Michigan, Michigan State University, the Cranbrook Academy of Science, the Smithsonian Institution and the New York Botanical Garden—and Mrs. Boydston, encouraged by her success with the delicate plants, conducted many other successful hybridizing experiments when her farm, Fernwood, became part of a 100-acre nature and garden preserve open to the public.

The actual mechanics of creating a fern hybrid are simple. Place the sexual parts of the prothallia of two ferns that you have judged potentially capable of producing an interesting hybrid in such proximity that the sperm of one can swim over the leaflike surface of the other and toward its female organ. This involves severing the male, or pointed, end of one prothallium and the indented, or female, end of another. Since you cannot be sure beforehand that the eggs have not already been fertilized by the sperm present on the prothallium to begin with, it is best to trim the tiny leaf when it is just becoming clearly defined and has not been allowed to develop for more than two months.

If such surgical intervention seems a bother, you can simply plant the prothallia as close to each other as you can get them and let the contending factions of sperm fight it out. For this haphazard method to succeed, you must keep the surfaces of the plantlets as slitheringly watered as possible short of drowning them or creating drainage problems in their container.

WATCHING AND WAITING

With either method, bring the new hybrids to maturity exactly as you would nonhybrids, with one or two mass transplantings before they are set into individual pots. Of course, you will not even be able to tell whether you have hybrids or not until the plants bear mature fronds, which may take a year and a half. But fern propagators have to be patient. And eventually there will be clusters of feathery new plants, some perhaps of varieties that never before had existed on earth—and some perhaps of a size, shape or color so extraordinary that the wait is well rewarded.

ROOTING A TREE-FERN TRUNK

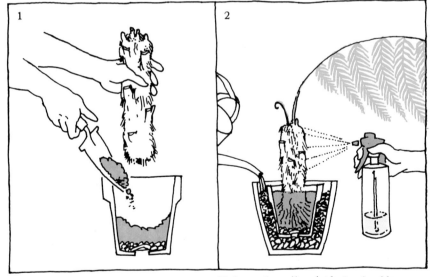

To plant a tree fern, bury the bottom third of the trunk in potting soil with the old leaf bases pointing up. Use a pot at least 6 inches larger than the trunk's diameter. Firm the soil and water the plant thoroughly.

To keep the soil moist but not soggy, set the pot on gravel inside a larger pot and stuff sphagnum moss between them. Keep the moss damp and mist the trunk daily. Set in a warm place, 65° to 75°, until roots form.

An illustrated encyclopedia of ferns 5

Most people still grow ferns in the traditional manner, as decorative potted house plants, but in recent years these plants have found wider use—in terrariums, hanging baskets, garden beds, trees, pockets along masonry walls, aquariums, even as vines on stakes. Growing recommendations for all these purposes, indoors and out, are provided in the encyclopedia pages following. The entries specify the ideal conditions. Ferns generally require special attention to their needs, and although most will tolerate slight variations from the recommendations, results may not be the same. For example, ferns can be maintained at lower levels of humidity than those indicated, but growth will be slower and less luxuriant.

One factor that greatly affects fern growth is soil acidity. If peat moss is used in the soil mix it will increase acidity, as is desirable for most ferns. Leaf mold is preferred over peat moss as a soil additive, however, and it can either increase or decrease acidity, depending on the leaves used to make it. With either peat moss or leaf mold, test for acidity and adjust it by including bone meal, sulfur or limestone as necessary *(pages 32-33)*.

Many of the ferns listed are tropical species and can be grown outdoors in the United States only in certain humid areas of the South. Suitable climate zones, keyed to the map on page 146, are specified in the entries. In other parts of the country, such ferns are kept in pots indoors over the winter, then moved out to a patio after the last frost, dates for which are given on page 147.

The encyclopedia listing in this volume includes a great many alternate names for the same plant because fern nomenclature is a matter of great dispute among authorities. The botanical names used here are those given in the second edition of *Dictionary of Gardening,* published by the Royal Horticultural Society of England, which is the standard adhered to in all volumes in the TIME-LIFE Encyclopedia of Gardening.

Ferns are more than just green plants with lacy foliage. Whether round-leaved button ferns, white-banded brake ferns or tough, leathery staghorns, they offer an incredible variety of sizes, colors and textures.

A

ACROSTICHUM

A. aureum (leather fern); *A. daneaefolium* (giant fern, swamp fern)

A native of both fresh-water swamps and salty marshes in the tropics, the leather fern is a robust, imposing plant that grows 3 to 8 feet high. It grows luxuriantly in climates with high humidity, such as that of the Florida Keys. Smooth, stiff stalks rise in a tight spiral from a stout, scaly root to carry an arching sprawl of fronds, each with 12 or more tough, dark green pointed leaflets 6 to 10 inches long. The fertile spore-bearing leaflets are at the tip of each frond and are smaller than the sterile leaflets below them. Spore cases cover the undersides of the fertile leaflets with a fuzzy brown coating.

The giant fern resembles the leather fern in appearance, but it is taller, growing 5 to 13 feet high, and all of the leaflets on its fertile fronds bear spores.

HOW TO GROW. Outdoors, grow these ferns in Zones 9 and 10, choosing a boggy location in open to light shade. In preparing a new bed, use a mixture of 1 part garden loam, 1 part builder's sand and 2 parts peat moss or leaf mold: a pH of 5.5 to 6.5 is best. Remove mature fronds from the plants when they begin to yellow.

Indoors, grow the leather fern or the giant fern in bright indirect or curtain-filtered sunlight (400 foot-candles) with night temperatures of 60° to 70°, daytime temperatures of 75° to 80°, and 60 per cent or more humidity. Plant either in a soil mix that is equal parts packaged potting soil, peat moss or leaf mold, and 1 part builder's sand, adding 2 tablespoons of bone meal to each gallon of mix. Feed twice during the spring and summer growing season, using fish emulsion diluted to half the strength recommended on the label. Treat either fern as an aquatic plant and keep the soil very wet by standing the pot in a water-filled saucer. Since warm, wet conditions encourage bacterial growth, replace the water in the saucer every few days and use sterile soil when repotting. Propagate from spores, which mature the year round.

ACTINIOPTERIS

A. australis, also called *A. semiflabellata*

Unlike most ferns, this one has adapted to dry growing conditions. It is a challenge for the gardener, for experimentation is needed to achieve the right combination of temperature, low humidity and soil moisture to cultivate it. The short stem branches sideways, sending up dense clumps of 4- to 10-inch fronds resembling tiny fan-palm leaves. This glossy, flat foliage is evenly forked into numerous toothpick-slim leaflets that radiate from the point where they join the stalk.

HOW TO GROW. Grow this fern outdoors in Zone 10, planting it in open shade in a well-drained site among rocks or in a separate bed where the barely moist condition it requires can be provided; overwatering quickly kills it. In preparing new beds, use 1 part garden loam, 1 part builder's sand and 2 parts leaf mold or peat moss. A pH of 6.0 to 7.0 is best.

Indoors in a pot or open terrarium, give it a minimum temperature of 60° at night and a humidity level of 50 per cent or less. Provide very bright indirect or curtain-filtered sunlight (800 foot-candles). Plant it in a potting mix that is 1 part peat moss or leaf mold, 1 part builder's sand and 2 parts perlite or vermiculite. Do not fertilize newly purchased or repotted plants for six months; feed established plants twice a year during the spring and summer growing season using fish emulsion diluted to half the strength recommended on the label. Keep the soil barely moist during the growing season, even drier during the winter months when the plant is dormant. Avoid moisture fluctuations. If you use a clay

LEATHER FERN
Acrostichum aureum

pot, place the potted plant inside a larger pot with the same soil mix between pots to help keep moisture uniform. Avoid getting water on the fronds. Propagate either from spores or by dividing the established plants. Outdoors, set divisions 1 foot apart to allow room for the fern to spread.

ADDER'S FERN See *Polypody*
ADDER'S-TONGUE FERN See *Ophioglossum*

ADIANTUM

A. capillus-veneris (southern maidenhair, Venus's maidenhair); *A. hispidulum* (rosy maidenhair, rough maidenhair); *A. macrophyllum; A. pedatum* (northern maidenhair, five-finger fern); *A. peruvianum* (silver-dollar fern); *A. raddianum,* also called *A. cuneatum* (delta maidenhair); *A. tenerum* (delicate maidenhair); *A. trapeziforme* (diamond maidenhair)

Maidenhair ferns are surrounded by legend. Some hold that the fern has power to restore, thicken or even curl hair, and according to a German tale, this type of plant originated when a maiden fell over a cliff after her lover turned into a wolf; a spring appeared where she fell and her hair turned into a fern. Today these ferns are especially prized for their delicate, airy foliage growing singly or in tufts along slender, branching stems. Tiny leaf buds unfurl into wedge-shaped green leaflets, ¼ to ½ inch across, that are carried on wiry, glossy black stalks.

The southern maidenhair sends up tufts of elongated oval fronds 6 to 20 inches long that form lacy, drooping canopies of thin, almost translucent evergreen leaflets. Rosy maidenhair forms dense clumps of 8- to 16-inch evergreen fronds. The tiny leaf buds and young leaflets are rose colored, turning green as they mature. *A. macrophyllum* grows a foot tall with 3-inch leaflets. The 10- to 20-inch stalks of the northern maidenhair fern carry 8- to 15-inch circular or horseshoe-shaped fronds parallel to the ground. The leaflets are green when young, turning blue-green when mature. The fronds die back after frost but the plant survives. The silver-dollar fern has enormous oval leaflets 3 to 4 inches long and so wide at their bases that the leaflet pairs overlap where they join the stalk. Young growth is red like that of rosy maidenhair. Delta maidenhair ferns are evergreens 9 to 18 inches high with stiff, erect fronds that are used by florists for cut greens. The variety *variegatum* has streaks of white on its green leaflets. The small variety Pacific Maid has large, satiny leaflets, each divided into two or three segments that crowd one another and overlap to give the fern a thick, fluffy appearance. The basic species of the delicate maidenhair fern is seldom grown, but *A. tenerum wrightii,* the fan maidenhair, is a popular evergreen variety with upright, gracefully arching fronds up to 20 inches long. The fan-shaped, overlapping leaflets turn from pink to light green. Diamond maidenhair grows 1½ to 3 feet tall; its leaflets are diamond shaped, 2 inches long and ¾ inch wide.

HOW TO GROW. Outdoors, grow the northern maidenhair fern in Zones 3-8; the southern, rosy and delta maidenhairs in Zones 7-10; and the silver-dollar fern, *A. macrophyllum,* the fan maidenhair and the diamond maidenhair in Zones 9 and 10. Choose barely moist locations in light shade. Southern and fan maidenhairs grow best in more alkaline soils with a pH of 7.0 to 8.0; tuck them into shady moist pockets among limestone rocks, along masonry walls or next to walks. All of the others grow best in acid soils with a pH of 5.5 to 6.5; use them in rock gardens or as border plants. In preparing new beds, use 1 part garden loam, 1 part builder's sand and 2 parts leaf mold or peat moss. For southern and fan maidenhairs, add 2 tablespoons of ground limestone per cu-

Actiniopteris australis

SOUTHERN MAIDENHAIR
Adiantum capillus-veneris

For climate zones and frost dates, see maps, pages 146-147.

ROSY MAIDENHAIR
Adiantum hispidulum

NORTHERN MAIDENHAIR
Adiantum pedatum

PACIFIC MAID MAIDENHAIR
Adiantum raddianum 'Pacific Maid'

FAN MAIDENHAIR
Adiantum tenerum wrightii

bic foot of soil. Remove yellowed fronds from evergreen species in fall and winter; remove dead fronds from the deciduous northern maidenhair in early spring, just before new growth unfolds.

Indoors, maidenhairs do best as terrarium plants because they need 60 per cent or more humidity to thrive, though rosy maidenhair will tolerate less. They can also be grown in uncovered pots in such humid rooms as kitchens and bathrooms. Maidenhair ferns do best in bright, indirect sunlight. Provide temperatures of 50° to 60° at night and 70° to 80° by day. Keep the ferns moist but not soggy and water less during the winter resting periods. Maidenhair ferns do best when their roots crowd their pots. When repotting, select a pot only one size larger or prune the roots severely and reuse the same pot. Use a mixture of 1 part packaged potting soil, 1 part peat moss or leaf mold and 1 part builder's sand. Add 2 tablespoons of bone meal to each gallon of soil mix; also add 1 tablespoon of ground limestone per gallon of mix for southern or fan maidenhairs. If older clumps in the center of a pot die, carefully cut away the dead portion and fill the hole with soil mix to avoid immediate repotting. Fertilize twice a year during the growing season, using fish emulsion diluted to half the strength recommended on the label. Remove older fronds as they yellow. Shriveling of young fronds indicates a need for higher humidity.

Propagate by division or by sowing spores. Divide and transplant in spring as new growth begins, placing new plants or divisions 1 to 2 feet apart in the garden. Southern maidenhair, rosy maidenhair and delta maidenhair ferns grow quickly from spores, producing plants that are ready for 2½-inch pots in a year. Delta maidenhair, in particular, reproduces so easily from spores that it soon forms colonies of young plants when grown outdoors.

AGLAOMORPHA See *Polypodium*
ALLOSORUS See *Cryptogramma*

ALSOPHILA

A. cooperi, also called *Sphaeropteris cooperi, A. australis* (Australian tree fern, Cooper tree fern)

The Australian tree fern is a spectacular plant in its native Australia where its trunklike stem grows 15 to 20 feet high, sprouting huge, fan-shaped fronds that spread as much as 20 feet in diameter. Cultivated plants are usually 6 to 8 feet high, but under ideal growing conditions the Australian tree fern can add a foot or more of growth each year. *A. cooperi* Brentwood is an especially fast-growing variety. The hairy scales found on the trunk and at the base of the fronds may cause skin irritation.

HOW TO GROW. Outdoors, grow the Australian tree fern in Zones 9 and 10 where night temperatures are at least 10° cooler than day. Choose a moist, well-drained site protected from strong winds, in open shade or full sun; do not plant under trees where water will drip into the crown. A new garden bed can be prepared using 1 part garden loam, 1 part builder's sand and 2 parts peat moss or leaf mold. A pH of 6.0 to 7.0 is best.

Grow the Australian tree fern indoors in curtain-filtered sunlight or very bright indirect sunlight such as that reflected from light walls (800 foot-candles). Provide night temperatures of 50° to 60°, day temperatures of 70° to 80° and humidity of 60 per cent or more. For best results, plant the fern in a mixture of equal parts packaged potting soil, builder's sand and peat moss or leaf mold; add 2 tablespoons of bone meal to each gallon of this mix. Keep the soil moist at all times and allow it to dry slightly between waterings. Do

AUSTRALIAN TREE FERN
Alsophila cooperi

For climate zones and frost dates, see maps, pages 146-147.

PINE FERN
Anemia adiantifolia

FLOWERING FERN
Anemia phyllitidis

not feed newly potted or newly purchased plants for three months; fertilize established plants twice during the spring and summer growing season with fish emulsion diluted to half the strength recommended on the label. Plants can stay in the same containers for a long time, but growth is slow. Repot root-bound ferns in spring as the new young fronds uncurl at the top of the trunk. Remove yellowed fronds from the plant by cutting them off close to the trunk. Propagate the Australian tree fern from its spores, which shower from the older, lower fronds.

ALSOPHILA See also *Cyathea*
AMERICAN ROCK BRAKE See *Cryptogramma*
AMERICAN TREE FERN See *Dryopteris*
AMERICAN WATER FERN See *Ceratopteris*

ANEMIA

A. adiantifolia (pine fern); *A. phyllitidis* (flowering fern)

What look like flower buds on these small ferns are actually modified leaflets bearing clusters of spore cases that resemble tiny berries when immature and tan flowers when ripe. The pine fern has triangular fronds 10 to 20 inches long with fine, airy sterile leaflets, which are carried on wiry, slightly hairy stalks that rise from a stout scaly rootstock. The slow-growing flowering fern has sterile fronds 1 to 2 feet long with broad, pointed oval leaflets.

HOW TO GROW. The pine fern and flowering fern grow outdoors only in Zone 10, doing best in light to open shade. Choose sites that are generally moist but that dry slightly between waterings. In preparing a new bed, use a mixture of 1 part garden loam, 1 part builder's sand and 2 parts leaf mold or peat moss. A pH of 5.5 to 6.5 is best.

Indoors, keep them in bright or very bright indirect sunlight or curtain-filtered sunlight (400 to 800 foot-candles) where temperatures are 60° or 70° at night, 75° to 80° by day and humidity is 60 per cent or more. Plant in a mixture of equal parts of packaged potting soil, peat moss and builder's sand, adding 2 tablespoons of bone meal per gallon of mix. Allow the soil to dry slightly between waterings. Do not fertilize newly purchased or repotted plants for six months; feed established plants twice a year during the growing season, using fish emulsion diluted to half the strength recommended on the label. Remove fronds as they yellow and die. Propagate by planting spores or by dividing the roots; set new divisions 1 foot apart outdoors.

ANGOLA STAGHORN FERN See *Platycerium*
ANISOGONIUM See *Diplazium*

ANOGRAMMA

A. chaerophylla

This small terrarium fern, less than a foot tall, is unusual because it is an annual fern with a perennial prothallium, the tiny plantlet that grows from a spore and, through sexual union, gives rise to a new fern plant. Most ferns live many years, and in most fern life cycles, the prothallium disappears as soon as it achieves its purpose. In this species, however, the mature fern lives only one season, dying completely after it has dispersed its spores; its prothallia not only create new ferns for the next season, but also put out new prothallium buds on short stalks that eventually create other new ferns. *A. chaerophylla* has wide, triangular fronds growing in dense clumps. The thin leaflets are divided into fine segments and the spore cases form along the veins on the undersides of the leaves.

HOW TO GROW. This *Anogramma* fern is best grown in a

terrarium in bright indirect or curtain-filtered sunlight (400 foot-candles). Minimum temperatures of 45° to 50° at night and 65° by day are recommended. Humidity of 60 per cent or more is ideal. Plant in a mixture of 1 part garden loam, 1 part peat moss or leaf mold, and 1 part builder's sand, adding 2 tablespoons of bone meal per gallon of mix. Keep the plant constantly moist but never soggy. New ferns can be fed once as their growth first appears using fish emulsion or another liquid house-plant fertilizer diluted to half the strength recommended on the label. *A. chaerophylla* grows rapidly during its single season and can be propagated easily from spores, reproducing itself readily in terrariums.

ARACHNIODES See *Polystichum*
ASPIDOTIS See *Pellaea*

ASPLENIUM

A. bulbiferum (mother fern, mother spleenwort); *A. nidus* (bird's-nest fern); *A. platyneuron* (ebony spleenwort); *A. trichomanes* (maidenhair spleenwort); *A. viviparum,* also called *A. daucifolium* (Mauritius mother fern) (all also called spleenwort)

Spleenworts are a widely distributed, diverse group of ferns. These five easily grown species offer a broad choice of size and appearance. The mother fern and the bird's-nest fern are medium-sized tropical species, while the ebony and maidenhair spleenworts are small ferns for colder climates.

The mother fern's feathery, arching fronds, 1 to 2 feet long and up to 9 inches wide, are on wiry, dark, scaly stalks that rise from a short, creeping stem. The soft, feathery leaflets of the sterile fronds are broader than those on spore-bearing fronds of mature plants, providing an unusual combination of distinctly different shapes. Tiny bulblets form on the upper surface of its fronds and develop into miniature fern plants. Use it outdoors along borders or as a pot plant indoors.

The bird's-nest fern has thin, leathery, tonguelike fronds with wavy edges that make it a dramatic accent plant. The variety *crispafolium* has deeply ruffled leaves. As a house plant, the bird's-nest fern rarely exceeds 12 to 15 inches in height, but given more warmth and humidity, it can grow to 4 feet. Glossy green with prominent, polished ribs down their centers, the fronds form a bird's-nest shape rising from a crown covered with hairy dark scales. The stem is erect and stumpy. Leaf buds grow slowly up through the shaggy stem cover, and as the new center leaves unfold, the older ones gradually die. Covered spore cases appear only on larger plants in a herringbone pattern on the leaves' undersides.

The ebony spleenwort sends up erect, slender, 8- to 15-inch-long, ladder-like fertile fronds that taper at both ends. The dark green fertile fronds rise first but die down after frost. The more numerous light green sterile fronds appear later, growing outward and almost flat on the surface of the ground. Shorter and broader than the fertile fronds, they stay green year round. This fern is good for rock gardens and wall niches outdoors or rocky terrariums indoors.

Another fern to plant between rocks is the maidenhair spleenwort, which spreads its sterile, evergreen fronds close to the ground in rosettes rising from shallow, black, scaly stems. The slender 5- to 6-inch fronds have rounded leaflets paired along dark, lustrous stalks. These ¼-inch leaflets have slightly toothed upper edges and sometimes overlap. The green fertile fronds are more erect than the sterile fronds and rise later in the summer. Their leaflets drop off in early winter, leaving bare stalks standing on the plant.

Mauritius mother fern has extremely narrow leaflets on 10- to 15-inch fronds that cascade gracefully over the sides

Anogramma chaerophylla

MOTHER FERN
Asplenium bulbiferum

For climate zones and frost dates, see maps, pages 146-147.

BIRD'S-NEST FERN
Asplenium nidus

EBONY SPLEENWORT
Asplenium platyneuron

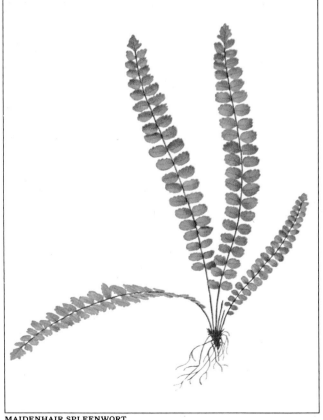

MAIDENHAIR SPLEENWORT
Asplenium trichomanes

LADY FERN
Athyrium filix-femina

of pots and hanging baskets. Like the mother fern it produces bulblets along its frond surfaces.

HOW TO GROW. The mother fern, Mauritius mother fern and the bird's-nest fern can be grown outdoors in Zones 7-10, the ebony and maidenhair spleenworts in Zones 3-8. Outdoors, grow these five ferns in deep shade in locations where the soil is constantly moist but well drained. The ebony and maidenhair spleenworts will tolerate short dry spells, and in very moist locations they withstand full sun. In preparing a new bed, use a mixture of 1 part garden loam, 1 part builder's sand and 2 parts peat moss or leaf mold for the mother fern, the Mauritius mother fern and bird's-nest fern, which grow best with a pH of 6.0 to 7.0. For ebony and maidenhair spleenworts, which thrive at a pH of 7.0 to 8.0, add 2 tablespoons of ground limestone per cubic foot of soil mix. Do not trim off live fronds during the winter dormant period or you will stimulate growth at the wrong season.

Indoors, grow these ferns in a low level of indirect light such as that in a north window (150 foot-candles). The mother fern, Mauritius mother fern and bird's-nest fern do best when temperatures are 50° to 60° at night and 70° to 80° by day. Cooler temperatures of 45° to 55° at night and 65° to 75° by day are ideal for the ebony and maidenhair spleenworts. All five ferns do best when the humidity is 60 per cent or more. Keep the soil moist but never soggy, and water less during winter resting periods. For mother fern or bird's-nest fern, use a soil mix of equal parts packaged potting soil, builder's sand and peat moss or leaf mold, adding 2 tablespoons of bone meal to each gallon of mix. For ebony and maidenhair spleenworts, add a tablespoon of ground limestone to each gallon. Do not fertilize newly purchased or repotted plants for six months; feed established plants twice a year during the growing season using fish emulsion diluted to half the strength recommended on the label. Keep the ferns neat and healthy by cutting off dead fronds year round.

All of these ferns can be propagated from spores and all but the bird's-nest fern can be increased by stem division. Propagate the mother fern and Mauritius mother fern by removing the buds that crowd the fronds in spring and summer and pinning them to the surface of sterilized potting soil until the new ferns are firmly rooted.

ASPLENIUM See *Ceterach* and *Phyllitis*

ATHYRIUM
A. filix-femina (lady fern); *A. goeringianum pictum,* also called *A. niponicum pictum* (Japanese painted fern); *A. pycnocarpon* (glade fern); *A. thelypterioides* (silvery glade fern)

Athyriums are graceful medium-to-large ferns with a great variety of leaflet shapes and colors. They are deciduous, their fronds yellowing or withering by late summer even in warm climates. Their fronds rise from stout, shallow, creeping stems that are usually covered with dark scales. The spore cases appear in a herringbone pattern on the undersides of the crowded leaflets.

The lady fern is a feathery, lacy species that comes in so many forms that its cultivated varieties defy neat classification. These ferns spread slowly, sending up oval to triangular fronds, 3 feet long and up to 15 inches wide. The smooth stalks are light green or light red. The thin, yellow-green, finely toothed leaflets turn deeper green as they mature.

The frond stalks and the ribs down the center of each of the Japanese painted fern leaflets are dark red, the red blending subtly into the gray-green leaflets. This fern also spreads slowly, and its compact growth makes it a good choice for border or foundation plantings. Its coiled new

For climate zones and frost dates, see maps, pages 146-147.

JAPANESE PAINTED FERN
Athyrium goeringianum pictum

GLADE FERN
Athyrium pycnocarpon

SILVERY GLADE FERN
Athyrium thelypterioides

MOSQUITO FERN
Azolla filiculoides

growth, the crosiers, emerges quite late in spring, but it continues to unfold into tufts of 2-foot, spear-shaped fronds throughout the summer. Spores are carried on the backs of the leaflets over the whole surface of each frond.

The glade fern, also slow to spread, is a tall, slender fern whose fronds are a light, brilliant green at first, darkening through the summer and turning russet toward fall. The glade fern's 3- to 4-foot fronds are produced close together on a short creeping stem that stays buried in the ground. Both sterile and fertile fronds bear 3-inch-long, tapering leaflets about ½ inch wide. The sterile fronds, which appear first in spring and continue to rise all summer, are broader and more arching than the fertile fronds, which rise later. The fertile fronds have longer stalks, are more erect and have narrower leaflets than the sterile ones.

The silvery glade fern has leaflets with deeply lobed edges that give it a feathery appearance like that of the lady fern, which it also resembles in growth habit. Silvery spore cases give a sheen to the backs of the leaflets. The 3-foot, lance-shaped fronds are yellow-green at first, changing to deep green, then to russet in late summer. The sterile fronds, growing on the outside of the fern's loose clumps, appear in spring. The taller fertile ones come up in the summer. The prominent, silvery spore cases turn blue as they mature.

HOW TO GROW. Grow athyriums outdoors, in Zones 3-8 in light to open shade. Choose sites that are consistently moist, even slightly wet, but never soggy. In preparing new beds for lady ferns, Japanese painted ferns or silvery glade ferns use a mixture of 1 part garden loam, 1 part builder's sand and 2 parts peat moss or leaf mold; a pH of 5.5 to 6.5 is best. For glade ferns, add 1 to 2 tablespoons of ground limestone per cubic foot of mix for a pH of 7.0 to 8.0. Remove dead fronds in spring just before new growth begins to unfurl.

Although athyriums are not house plants, they may be grown from spores indoors until they are large enough to transplant outside. Indoors, provide bright to very bright indirect or curtain-filtered sunlight (400 to 800 foot-candles). Give them temperatures of 45° to 55° at night, 65° to 75° by day, and humidity as close to 60 per cent as possible. For all but glade ferns, use a soil mix of equal parts of packaged potting soil, peat moss or leaf mold, and builder's sand, adding 2 tablespoons of bone meal per gallon of mix. For glade ferns, add 1 tablespoon of ground limestone to each gallon of this mix. Do not fertilize newly purchased or repotted plants for six months; feed established plants twice a year during the growing season, using fish emulsion diluted to half the strength recommended on the label. Keep the soil moist at all times but never soggy, and water less during the winter resting period.

Lady ferns can be propagated by root division and are particularly easy to raise from spores. Spores will grow into plants large enough for 2½-inch pots in a year. They can also be propagated by layering: pegging a lower frond to the surface of the soil until new roots form.

ATHYRIUM See also *Diplazium*
AUSTRALIAN BRAKE FERN See *Pteris*
AUSTRALIAN TREE FERN See *Alsophila*

AZOLLA
A. caroliniana; A. filiculoides (both called mosquito fern, duckweed fern)

These ferns carpet the surface of warm, sluggish waters with dense mats of ¼- to 1-inch plants that reputedly prevent mosquito breeding, hence the common name of mosquito fern. Natives of South America, they have escaped from cultivation in this country and grow wild in California and from Maryland and northern Virginia south to Florida. *A. caroliniana* has double rows of round to oval stemless leaves, less than $^1/_{16}$ inch long, that overlap one another like scales. Threadlike rootlets dangle from nodes where the rootstock branches. *A. filiculoides* has narrower, pointed leaves. Mosquito ferns, which are often grown in garden pools, appear red in sunlight, green in the shade. They produce separate male and female spores, instead of single spores that carry the characteristics of both sexes, as ferns normally do.

HOW TO GROW. Mosquito ferns can be grown in Zones 7-10, in warm, still water that contains some organic matter and has a pH of 6.5 to 7.0. Grow them indoors in mud or saucers of water in a terrarium, or in a home aquarium. Give them very bright indirect or curtain-filtered sunlight (800 foot-candles). Mosquito ferns will quickly weaken and die in a terrarium or aquarium that does not receive bright light. Air temperatures that range from 50° at night to 80° by day are best, and a water temperature of 70° to 75° is ideal for their growth. Propagate the mosquito ferns by divison, severing rooted sections and floating them on the water surface. They spread rapidly and can be hard to contain.

B

BALL FERN See *Davallia*
BEAD FERN See *Onoclea*
BEAR'S-FOOT FERN See *Humata*
BIRD'S-NEST FERN See *Asplenium*
BIRD'S-NEST FERN, CLIMBING See *Polypodium*
BLACK TREE FERN See *Cyathea*
BLADDER FERN See *Cystopteris*

BLECHNUM

B. brasiliense; B. gibbum; B. occidentale (hammock fern); *B. spicant* (deer fern)

The *Blechnum* species are tropical ferns noted for their durability as house plants. Their coarse, stiff fronds also make them attractive accent plants outdoors in warm climates. *B. brasiliense* is a dwarf tree fern having fronds 3 to 4 feet long and a foot wide on short stalks. The fronds are set at a sharp angle to the stalk, forming compact bushy crowns. *B. gibbum,* another dwarf tree fern, has a loose, spreading crown of fronds atop a 3- to 5-foot trunk that is formed of frond stalks and masses of aerial roots.

The colorful hammock fern sends up pink, tightly coiled young fronds, or crosiers, that are covered with brown scales. The copper color of the tufts of new young fronds, spaced along the hammock fern's creeping stem, contrasts with the dark green of older clumps. Sterile evergreen fronds, 12 to 15 inches long and 4 inches wide, have undivided leaflets that grow closer together toward the tops of the lance-shaped fronds. The fertile fronds are similar but narrower and die back each year. The spore cases grow on the backs of leaflets like paired narrow brown ribbons.

The evergreen deer fern has numerous sterile fronds growing in rosettes along a short, creeping stem. The tough fronds (the British common name is hard fern) grow up to 2 feet high, with dark green linear leaflets that are rounded at the tips and paler beneath. A few fertile fronds rise to 3 feet tall from the center of each cluster of sterile fronds. With narrow leaflets just wide enough for two rows of spore cases, they resemble coarse combs. They die down each year.

HOW TO GROW. *B. brasiliense, B. gibbum* and the hammock fern grow best in Zones 9 and 10 in evenly moist sites with light to open shade. However, they will tolerate drier soils and will grow in alternate sun and shade if they receive

HAMMOCK FERN
Blechnum occidentale

DEER FERN
Blechnum spicant

For climate zones and frost dates, see maps, pages 146-147.

adequate moisture. The deer fern grows best in Zones 3-8 in consistently moist sites in deep shade. In preparing a new bed for any of these ferns, use a mixture of 1 part garden loam, 1 part builder's sand and 2 parts peat moss or leaf mold. A pH of 5.5 to 6.5 is best.

Indoors, provide bright to very bright indirect light or curtain-filtered sunlight (400 to 800 foot-candles) for *B. brasiliense, B. gibbum* or the hammock fern; give the deer fern a low level of indirect light such as that in a north window (150 foot-candles). Temperatures of 50° to 60° at night and 70° to 80° by day are ideal. Keep humidity as close to 60 per cent as possible. Use a soil mix that is equal parts of packaged potting soil, builder's sand and peat moss or leaf mold, adding 2 tablespoons of bone meal per gallon of mix. Do not fertilize newly purchased or repotted plants for six months; feed established plants twice a year during the growing season using fish emulsion diluted to half the strength recommended on the label. Keep the soil evenly moist but never soggy; water less during the winter resting period. When roots fill the pot, repot in spring as new growth begins, placing the fern in a pot one size larger.

Indoors, trim off dead fronds year round, but do not remove old fronds outdoors until new growth appears in spring. All these ferns can be propagated from spores at any season. The hammock fern and the deer fern can also be propagated by dividing plants; do this in spring so that the divisions have a whole growing season to become established.

BLUNT-LOBED CLIFF FERN See *Woodsia*
BLUNT-LOBED WOODSIA See *Woodsia*

BOTRYCHIUM

B. dissectum (cut-leaved grape fern, lacy leaf grape fern); *B. matricariaefolium* (daisy-leaf grape fern); *B. multifidum* (leather grape fern); *B. virginianum* (rattlesnake fern)

Unlike most ferns, the botrychiums do not have scaly, creeping stems, and they do not send up tight coils of new growth. Their unbranched stems are fleshy and smooth and are buried underground. A single folded sterile frond pushes straight up from the soil each spring, then bends, opening upward. Spore cases in large clusters at the tips of fertile stalks give rise to the common names of the various species. Fertile stalks do not appear in young plants, and a mature plant may not produce one each year. After the spores mature, the fertile stalk withers and disappears. Botrychiums are best bought from commercial sources. They are difficult to transplant from the wild because of the special relationship between their fleshy roots and soil fungi. Botrychiums are generally not used as indoor pot plants.

The cut-leaved grape fern grows to a height of 6 to 15 inches with a triangular frond that changes from green to bronze in fall and remains standing throughout winter. Yellow spore cases and a sterile frond resembling a daisy's leaf characterize the deciduous 2- to 12-inch daisy-leaf grape fern. The 4- to 15-inch leather grape fern's evergreen frond takes a variety of shapes but is always tough and coarse textured. The rattlesnake fern, with a height of 6 to 20 inches, is the largest and also the most common of the botrychium species. Its deciduous sterile frond is lacier and thinner than those of the other species.

HOW TO GROW. Botrychium ferns grow in light shade in Zones 3-9. The plants are not easy to grow; avoid direct sun or they will disappear. Plant them in soil that is rich and loose. In preparing a new bed, use a mixture of equal parts of garden loam, builder's sand and leaf mold or peat moss. Soil pH should be 6.0 to 7.0. Keep the soil evenly moist. If you

RATTLESNAKE FERN
Botrychium virginianum

transplant from the wild, dig a large ball of earth to protect the 2-inch-deep fleshy stem and replant at the same depth.

BOULDER FERN See *Dennstaedtia*
BRACKEN FERN See *Pteridium*
BRAKE, AMERICAN ROCK See *Cryptogramma*
BRAKE, CRETAN or SPIDER See *Pteris*
BRAKE FERN See *Pteridium* and *Pteris*
BRAKEROOT See *Polypodium*
BRAMBLE FERN See *Hypolepis*
BRISTLE FERN See *Trichomanes*
BRITTLE BLADDER FERN See *Cystopteris*
BUCKLER FERN See *Dryopteris*
BULBLET BLADDER FERN See *Cystopteris*
BUTTON FERN See *Pellaea* and *Tectaria*

C

CALIFORNIA GOLDBACK FERN See *Pityrogramma*
CALIFORNIA SHIELD FERN See *Dryopteris*
CALLIPTERIS See *Diplazium*

CAMPTOSORUS
C. rhizophyllus (walking fern)

The evergreen walking fern is named for the unusual way it reproduces itself: tips of its spear-shaped fronds arch over, touch earth and take root again and again until the parent plant is surrounded by three and four generations that have "walked" to their new locations. In time, large tangled mats form. The slightly leathery, 6- to 12-inch fronds grow in a star-shaped tuft from the erect stem. In young plants, the fronds lie flat on the ground, but in older plants, they are upright and arching. The walking fern is rare in the wild but is occasionally found on limestone cliffs or in rocky woodlands in the Eastern United States. Use it outdoors in a rock garden or near damp rocks beside a pool or stream.

HOW TO GROW. The walking fern is difficult to establish in the garden. It grows best in open shade or alternate sun and shade in moist soil in Zones 3-8. Temperatures of 40° to 60° at night and 65° to 75° by day during the spring and summer are ideal. Plant it among rocks or in crevices, preferably in a mixture of 1 part garden loam, 1 part builder's sand and 2 parts peat moss or leaf mold. Add ground limestone, 1 to 2 tablespoons per cubic foot of soil, for a pH of 7.0 to 8.0.

Indoors, give the walking fern bright indirect light and temperatures ranging from 45° at night to 75° by day. This fern does best in humidity of 60 per cent, and is best grown in a terrarium. Keep it consistently moist, never soggy, and water less during the winter resting period. Use a soil mix with a pH of 7.0 to 8.0 that is equal parts packaged potting soil, builder's sand and leaf mold or peat moss, adding 2 tablespoons of bone meal and 1 tablespoon of ground limestone per gallon of mix. Do not fertilize newly purchased or repotted plants for six months; feed established plants twice a year during the growing season using fish emulsion diluted to half the strength recommended on the label. Trim dead fronds after new growth appears in spring. Propagate from spores or by cutting well-rooted new ferns from an older leaf's growing tip.

CAMPYLONEURUM See *Polypodium*
CARROT FERN See *Onychium*

CERATOPTERIS
C. pteridoides (American water fern); *C. thalictroides* (Oriental water fern, water sprite) (both called floating staghorn fern)

For climate zones and frost dates, see maps, pages 146-147.

WALKING FERN
Camptosorus rhizophyllus

ORIENTAL WATER FERN
Ceratopteris thalictroides

SCALE FERN
Ceterach officinarum

LACE FERN
Cheilanthes gracillima

These fast-growing aquatic ferns are edible, tasting like lettuce but slightly more nutty. Both are annuals found in quiet tropical waters all over the world, including the southeastern United States. They grow from a few inches across to 2 feet wide. The American water fern has broad triangular sterile fronds while those of the Oriental water fern are narrower, resembling parsley. The sterile fronds grow in rosettes with thick bunches of rootlets that hang down in the water when the ferns float. New fern buds sprout in the clefts of sterile leaflets. Mature fertile fronds, growing vertically up to 1 foot high, resemble brown, branched twigs. These ferns can be floated in an outdoor pool, planted along a muddy aquarium bottom or grown in a pot submerged up to its rim. When used as floating aquarium plants, their root masses offer young fish a safe hiding place.

HOW TO GROW. The American and Oriental water ferns grow well outdoors in light shade in Zone 10. Indoors, provide bright indirect or curtain-filtered sunlight (400 foot-candles). Air temperatures can range from 60° to 70° at night and 75° to 80° by day, but best growth results when air and water temperatures are between 68° and 78°. To grow in a pool, float the fern in soft water containing some organic matter. For an aquarium bottom or a pot, use a mix of equal parts packaged potting soil or garden loam, builder's sand and leaf mold or peat moss with an acid pH of 5.0 to 6.5.

Although these ferns die back in winter, new ferns grow from spores or from the leaf buds. These leaf buds float free when the parent plant withers, or they can be propagated by cutting them with small pieces of frond attached and pinning them to moist soil in a flowerpot. They can also be propagated from spores; sow as you would any other spores, but when seedlings appear, submerge the pot in water deep enough to cover the crowns. These water ferns can become weeds in ponds but they can be controlled by periodic thinning.

CERATOPTERIS See also *Pityrogramma*

CETERACH
C. aureum (rusty-back fern); *C. dalhousiae,* also called *Asplenium alternans; C. officinarum,* also called *Asplenium ceterach* (scale fern, also called rusty-back fern)

These plants have dense coatings of chaffy brown scales on the backs of their leathery fronds that help them retain moisture during extended dry spells. *C. aureum* has tufts of fronds 9 to 15 inches high and 2 inches wide. *C. dalhousiae* has 7- to 10-inch fronds with ½-inch lance-shaped leaflets. The scale fern's evergreen fronds, 4 to 6 inches long and 1 inch wide, are cut into ½-inch round-tipped leaflets. These leaflets roll inward and the fern appears dead during long dry spells, but they uncurl again after rain.

HOW TO GROW. Outdoors, these ferns grow best in light shade in Zones 3-8. Choose well-drained sites where they will stay just barely moist at all times. Fluctuations from bone dry to soggy can weaken and even kill them. If necessary, plant them alone where their special moisture needs can be met. Use a mixture of 1 part garden loam, 1 part leaf mold or peat moss, and 1 or 2 parts builder's sand. Add 2 tablespoons of ground limestone per cubic foot of soil for the scale fern, which grows best in alkaline soil with a pH of 7.0 to 8.0. *C. aureum* and *C. dalhousiae* need a pH of 5.5 to 6.5.

Indoors, provide bright indirect or curtain-filtered sunlight (400 foot-candles), temperatures ranging from 45° to 55° at night up to 65° to 75° by day, and humidity of 40 per cent or lower. Plant them in a mixture of 1 part packaged potting soil, 1 part leaf mold or peat moss, and 1 or 2 parts builder's sand; add 2 tablespoons of bone meal to each gallon of mix.

Add 1 tablespoon of ground limestone to each gallon of mix used for the scale fern. Place potted ferns inside a larger pot with the same soil mix between the pots to maintain uniform moisture, and keep the soil just barely moist at all times. Avoid getting water on the fronds. Do not feed newly purchased or repotted plants for six months; feed established plants twice a year during the growing season using fish emulsion diluted to half the strength recommended on the label. Propagate these ferns by sowing spores.

CHAIN FERN See *Woodwardia*

CHEILANTHES

C. gracillima (lace fern); *C. lanosa* (hairy lip fern); *C. tomentosa*, also called *C. fendleri*, *C. lanosa* (woolly lip fern)

These small, dainty ferns inhabit dry, rocky cliffs and ledges. All are evergreen. The woolly, hairy covering on the undersides of their leaflets helps them conserve moisture. In times of drought, the leaflets curl up, but they revive at the next rain. The thin 2- to 4-inch fronds of the lace fern rise in tufts from a short branching stem. The rare hairy lip fern has yellow-green to blue-green fronds, 6 to 8 inches long, that are carried on hairy stalks. The woolly lip fern is the hairiest of the three species and, like the hairy lip fern, it is rare in the wild. Its tiny leaflets are more deeply divided than those of the hairy lip fern and are covered underneath by dense mats of white hairs.

HOW TO GROW. Outdoors, these three ferns grow in Zones 3-8. The lace fern and the woolly lip fern grow best in open shade while the hairy lip fern is suited to deep shade. They require good drainage so that they are kept barely moist, even slightly dry, at all times. They are weakened by moisture fluctuations, and overwatering can kill them. To provide these exacting conditions, it may be necessary to plant them in a separate bed. Use a mixture of 1 part garden loam, 1 part leaf mold or peat moss, and 1 or 2 parts builder's sand with a pH of 5.5 to 6.5. Mulch to provide winter protection.

Indoors, provide very bright indirect or curtain-filtered sunlight (800 foot-candles) for the lace fern or the woolly lip fern, less for the hairy lip fern. Keep the soil barely moist and avoid moisture fluctuations. To help do this, place a potted fern inside a larger pot with soil mix between the two pots. Use a mixture of 1 part packaged potting soil, 1 part leaf mold or peat moss, and 1 or 2 parts builder's sand; add 2 tablespoons of bone meal per gallon of mix. Do not feed newly purchased or repotted plants for six months; feed established plants twice during the spring and summer growing season using fish emulsion diluted to half the strength recommended on the label. Propagate new plants by dividing their underground stems or by sowing spores.

CHEILANTHES See also *Pellaea*
CHRISTMAS FERN See *Polystichum*

CIBOTIUM

C. barometz (Scythian lamb); *C. glaucum,* also called *C. chamissoi* (Hawaiian tree fern, hapu); *C. schiedei* (Mexican tree fern)

These tree ferns are large, elegant plants that can be grown in pots while young but eventually must be set into large tubs and spacious settings. Scythian lamb, with fragrant, hairy 4- to 5-foot fronds, forms no trunk as other tree ferns do. It was once thought to be the "vegetable lamb" of medieval legend, a woolly animal-plant with a root attached to its navel. Although this legendary creature turned out to be a tree fern with a hairy stalk, the common name persists.

For climate zones and frost dates, see maps, pages 146-147.

HAIRY LIP FERN
Cheilanthes lanosa

HAWAIIAN TREE FERN
Cibotium glaucum

MEXICAN TREE FERN
Cibotium schiedei

AMERICAN ROCK BRAKE
Cryptogramma crispa

The Hawaiian species grows 15 feet tall in its native rain forest. Its fibrous trunk is covered with golden hairs and is crowned by a tuft of crinkled fronds up to 6 feet wide. The stout trunk is a core of a moisture-storing starch surrounded by a mass of aerial roots, enabling it to survive for some time when propped upright in water with rocks or pebbles.

The Mexican tree fern's fronds sprout rapidly from the base of the plant, but it grows so slowly in height that it is rarely seen with a trunk outside its native Mexico and Guatemala. There it may reach 15 feet, but in cultivation the fern usually grows 3 to 4 feet high with a shapely fountain of fronds 6 feet in diameter—the symmetrical shape makes it a favorite of florists for formal occasions.

HOW TO GROW. The Scythian lamb grows outdoors in Zone 10, the Hawaiian and Mexican tree ferns in Zones 9 and 10 in moist sites protected from strong winds. The Scythian lamb and the Mexican tree fern grow best in light shade; the Hawaiian tree fern is suited to open shade and will tolerate some direct sun if it is not too intense and if the soil is moist. Use a soil mix of equal parts garden loam, builder's sand and leaf mold or peat moss. A pH of 6.0 to 7.0 is best.

Indoors, provide bright indirect light (400 foot-candles) for the Scythian lamb and the Mexican tree fern. Give the Hawaiian tree fern curtain-filtered or very bright indirect sunlight such as that reflected from light walls (800 foot-candles). Night temperatures of 50° to 60°, day temperatures of 70° to 80°, and humidity of 60 per cent or higher are ideal. Use a soil mix of equal parts packaged potting soil, builder's sand and leaf mold or peat moss, adding 2 tablespoons of bone meal per gallon of mix. Do not feed newly purchased or repotted plants for six months; feed established plants twice during the spring and summer growing season using fish emulsion diluted to half the strength recommended on the label. Keep the soil evenly moist and water less during the winter resting period; too much moisture rots the roots.

The Hawaiian tree fern is sometimes sold in the continental United States as 1- to 4-foot sections of trunks. Select sections that are fresh, not shriveled or brown and too dry to plant. Plants establish themselves slowly, taking 2 to 3 months to develop good root systems and as long as a year to develop symmetrical crowns of four or five fronds. Do not get the trunk upside down—you can tell how it grew originally by looking for the stubs of fronds, which point upward. All of these ferns can be propagated from spores.

CINNAMON FERN See *Osmunda*
CLAW FERN, JAPANESE See *Onychium*
CLIFF BRAKE See *Pellaea*
CLIFF FERN See *Woodsia*
CLIMBING BIRD'S-NEST FERN See *Polypodium*
CLIMBING FERN See *Lygodium*
CLOVER FERN, WATER See *Marsilea*
COASTAL WOOD FERN See *Dryopteris*
COOPER TREE FERN See *Alsophila*
CRAPE FERN See *Todea*
CRESTED SHIELD FERN See *Dryopteris*
CRETAN BRAKE See *Pteris*

CRYPTOGRAMMA
C. crispa, also called *C. acrostichoides, Allosorus crispus* (American rock brake, parsley fern)

Close up, American rock brake bears only a slight resemblance to parsley. But it is easy to imagine how climbers, seeing dense patches of it from a distance as they scrambled up the barren mountain tops where it thrives, could have mistaken it for the familiar garden herb. This extremely hardy 6- to 8-inch fern crowds tufts of fronds closely along a scaly horizontal stem. Each stalk is twice the length of the leafy portion of each frond, and the sterile and fertile fronds form two tiers of foliage. Weaker sterile fronds grow first and spread their leafy foliage below the stiffer fertile ones. The edges of fertile leaflets roll back to cover the immature spore cases on the undersurfaces so that the leaflets appear podlike and narrower than sterile leaflets. The fronds brown and wither after frost.

HOW TO GROW. American rock brake grows well in rock gardens in Zones 3-8 in a moist but not wet location in light shade. It requires a coarse soil to do well. In preparing a new bed, use a mixture of 1 part garden loam, 1 part builder's sand and 2 parts leaf mold or peat moss, adding gravel or brick rubble if the location is not rocky enough. A pH of 5.5 to 6.5 is ideal. Trim dead fronds just before new growth appears in the spring. This fern seldom survives as a house plant. Propagate it by sowing spores, by transplanting wild seedlings or by dividing the horizontal stem.

CTENITIS See *Dryopteris*
CUP FERN, COMMON See *Dennstaedtia*
CUP GOLDILOCKS See *Trichomanes*
CUT-LEAVED GRAPE FERN See *Botrychium*

CYATHEA
C. arborea (West Indian tree fern); *C. dealbata,* also called *Alsophila tricolor* (silver tree fern); *C. medullaris,* also called *Sphaeropteris medullaris* (black tree fern, Sago tree fern, mamaku)

The West Indian, silver and black tree ferns bear tufts of feathery evergreen fronds atop stout treelike trunks. The trunk is covered with the bases of dead fronds and masses of aerial roots, forming a fibrous mat that holds moisture. In its native environment, the West Indian tree fern may grow 50 feet tall with crowns of fronds 6 feet in diameter. Under cultivation, it seldom grows taller than 15 feet outdoors, and indoor tub plants grow very slowly, producing 1½- to 2-foot fronds in five to six years. In its native New Zealand, the silver tree fern reaches 30 feet or more, but cultivated plants usually grow 10 to 20 feet tall with fronds that spread 6 to 12 feet. The wide oval-to-triangular fronds are green or yellow-green on top and white underneath. The black tree fern is the largest tree fern that will survive freezing. This New Zealand native grows to a height of 35 to 60 feet tall and has a black trunk 2½ feet thick. The enormous fronds, 8 to 20 feet long and up to 5 feet wide, have black ribs.

HOW TO GROW. The West Indian tree fern and the silver tree fern can be grown outdoors in Zone 10, the black tree fern in Zones 7-10. The West Indian tree fern grows best in Florida where day and night temperatures are about the same, while the silver and black tree ferns do best in California where nights are cooler than days. Grow them in well-drained soil in light to open shade, choosing a location protected from strong winds. In preparing a new bed, use a soil mix of 1 part garden loam, 1 part builder's sand and 2 parts peat moss or leaf mold. A pH of 6.0 to 7.0 is best.

Indoors provide bright indirect or curtain-filtered sunlight (400 foot-candles) for the West Indian and silver tree ferns; the black tree fern can have brighter illumination. Night temperatures of 60° to 70° for the West Indian tree fern and 50° to 60° for the silver or black tree ferns are ideal. Day temperatures of 70° to 80° and humidity of 60 per cent or more are recommended for all three species. Plant in a mixture of equal parts of packaged potting soil, builder's sand and leaf mold or peat moss, adding 2 tablespoons of bone

SILVER TREE FERN
Cyathea dealbata

For climate zones and frost dates, see maps, pages 146-147.

JAPANESE FELT FERN
Cyclophorus lingua

HOLLY FERN
Cyrtomium falcatum

meal to each gallon of mix. Keep the soil consistently moist but not soggy. Do not fertilize newly purchased or repotted plants for six months; feed established plants twice during the growing season, using fish emulsion diluted to half the strength recommended on the label. Outdoors or indoors, mist the trunk in summer to encourage good crown growth. Remove withered fronds in winter. Propagate from spores.

CYCLOPHORUS

C. lingua, also called *Niphobolus lingua, Pyrrosia lingua* (Japanese felt fern, tongue fern)

The common names of this plant are inspired by the dangling 9-inch fronds that resemble dark green tongues with fuzzy undersides. The backs of its leathery leaves are densely covered with hairs and scales. They rise about 1 inch apart along a creeping, red-scaled stem. The fern can be grown outdoors as a ground cover in a subtropical climate. Indoors, it is suited to display in a hanging basket or attached to a cork slab; it can also be grown in a pot.

HOW TO GROW. Outdoors, grow the Japanese felt fern in Zone 10 of Southern California and Florida. It grows best in light shade in moist, well-drained locations. In preparing a new bed, use 1 part garden loam, 1 part builder's sand and 2 parts leaf mold or peat moss. A pH of 6.0 to 7.0 is best.

Indoors, this air-growing, or epiphytic, plant grows best in bright indirect or curtain-filtered sunlight (400 foot-candles) with night temperatures of 60° to 70°, day temperatures of 75° to 80° and 50 to 60 per cent humidity. On cork slabs, anchor a moist mixture of sphagnum moss and tree fern fiber, then attach the fern to the bark with hardware cloth; keep constantly moist for several months while the plant is becoming established. In hanging baskets or pots, plant the Japanese felt fern in a mixture of 2 parts perlite or vermiculite, 1 part leaf mold or peat moss, and 1 part builder's sand. Fertilize once a month during the spring and summer growing season using fish emulsion diluted to half the strength recommended on the label. Keep the soil moist, but allow it to dry slightly between waterings, and water less during the winter resting period. When roots fill the pot or basket, repot the plant in spring, just as new growth begins. Propagate by dividing rhizomes (the thickened roots) or by sowing spores.

CYRTOMIUM

C. falcatum (holly fern, Japanese holly fern); *C. fortunei*

The holly fern, its leathery 3- to 5-inch leaflets dramatically impressive, is a good choice for beginners because it tolerates a wider range of conditions than most ferns. The lustrous fronds, up to 30 inches in length, spiral from an upright crown and arch gracefully, making this a good plant for pedestal display. The variety *C. falcatum caryotideum* has drooping leaflets with saw-toothed edges. *C. falcatum rochefordianum* has deeply toothed leaflets 2 inches wide. *C. fortunei*'s 2-foot fronds are not glossy. The narrow leaflets sometimes have ear-shaped lobes at their bases.

HOW TO GROW. These ferns grow outdoors in Zones 8-10 in a moist location in light shade, but they will tolerate more sun, drier soil and more exposed positions than other ferns. When preparing a new bed, use equal parts of garden loam, builder's sand and peat moss or leaf mold. A pH of 5.5 to 6.5 is recommended for all but *C. falcatum caryotideum;* add 1 tablespoon of ground limestone to each cubic foot of soil used for this fern to increase the pH to 7.0 to 8.0.

Indoors, keep these ferns moist and allow the soil to dry slightly between waterings. They grow best in bright indirect or curtain-filtered sunlight (400 foot-candles) with night temperatures of 50° to 60°, day temperatures of 70° to 80° and humidity as close to 60 per cent as possible. Repot root-bound plants in spring just as new fronds begin to uncurl. Use a mixture of equal parts packaged potting soil, builder's sand and peat moss or leaf mold. Add 2 tablespoons of bone meal to each gallon of this mixture for any of these ferns; also add 1 tablespoon of ground limestone to each gallon of soil mix used for *C. falcatum caryotideum*. Do not fertilize a newly purchased or repotted plant for six months; once established, feed twice during the spring and summer growing season with fish emulsion diluted to half the minimum strength recommended on the label. Propagate from spores.

CYSTOPTERIS

C. bulbifera (bulblet bladder fern); *C. fragilis* (fragile bladder fern, brittle bladder fern)

These delicate ferns with their thin, deeply cut, feathery fronds are among the first to unfurl in the spring garden. Their brittle, weak stalks and the hooded covers of the spore cases on the undersides of their fronds give them their several common names. The broad triangular fronds with smooth leaflets form dense crowns along the spreading stems, the rhizomes. The plants are deciduous; the foliage browns and dies after frost. The bulblet bladder fern's 1- to 2-foot arching fronds bear, in addition to spore cases, tiny buds on their upper sides, which can be planted to produce new ferns. The medium green, 10-inch fronds of the fragile bladder fern react to summer dry spells by turning reddish-brown, but they recover when they obtain moisture. These bladder ferns are good choices for rock gardens. They are not recommended as house plants because they do not do well in pots.

HOW TO GROW. Grow bulblet bladder and fragile bladder ferns in Zones 3-8 in deep shade. They grow well in moist pockets on a masonry wall, since they benefit from lime in their soil. When preparing a new bed outdoors, use 1 part garden loam, 1 part builder's sand and 2 parts leaf mold or peat moss; add 1 to 2 tablespoons ground limestone per cubic foot of soil for a pH of 7.0 to 8.0. Propagate by sowing spores or by dividing clumps in the spring; set divisions 1 foot apart outdoors. The bulblet bladder fern can also be propagated by removing and rooting the buds, which look like small green bulbs attached to the leaflets near the stalk, in late summer.

D

DAISY-LEAF GRAPE FERN See *Botrychium*

DAVALLIA

D. fejeensis (Fiji davallia); *D. mariesii,* also called *D. bullata,* (ball fern); *D. solida* (Polynesian davallia) (all also called davallia)

Davallias have hairy, scaly stems, or rhizomes, which resemble animal paws and creep over the edges of pots and encircle hanging baskets. In Victorian times it was fashionable to train deciduous species to wire shapes and to leave them hanging as indoor decorations after their fronds had dropped in the winter. In warm climates and sometimes indoors deciduous davallias may appear to be evergreen because older fronds do not drop off until the new growth is well under way. All davallias make good indoor or greenhouse pot plants and are used outdoors as ground covers. Since they are tropical air ferns that grow on the larger branches and trunks of trees, they are ideal for hanging baskets, which they will completely encircle with their fuzzy rhizomes.

The 12- to 18-inch Fiji davallia is an evergreen species with lacy foliage that lasts well in flower arrangements. The ball fern's broad 6- to 12-inch-long fronds, which rise from brown-scaled stems, have leathery leaflets. Outdoors in Zone

BULBLET BLADDER FERN
Cystopteris bulbifera

FRAGILE BLADDER FERN
Cystopteris fragilis

For climate zones and frost dates, see maps, pages 146-147.

FIJI DAVALLIA
Davallia fejeensis

HAY-SCENTED FERN
Dennstaedtia punctilobula

10, this deciduous fern drops its fronds after frost or in late winter before producing new growth. It is the davallia that is most often trained into shapes. The Polynesian davallia has broad, stiff 2-foot fronds, in contrast to the finely cut foliage that is typical of most davallias.

HOW TO GROW. These ferns can be grown outdoors only in Zone 10. Choose moist locations with very good drainage in deep to open shade. A new bed can be prepared using 1 part garden loam, 1 part builder's sand and 2 parts peat moss or leaf mold. A pH of 5.5 to 6.5 is best.

Indoors, all species grow as well in low light levels as in very bright light (150 to 800 foot-candles), but sunlight must be curtain filtered or indirect. They grow best when temperatures are 60° to 70° at night and 75° to 80° by day; the ball fern will thrive with night temperatures that are 10° cooler. Humidity of 50 per cent is recommended. Keep them moist, letting them dry slightly between waterings, and water sparingly during the winter resting period. These ferns can be grown on moist cork bark or osmunda fiber but they grow best in pots or hanging baskets in a mixture of 1 part perlite or vermiculite to 1 part peat moss or leaf mold; fertilize once a month during the spring and summer growing season using fish emulsion diluted to half the strength recommended on the label. When roots fill the pot or basket, repot in spring as new growth begins. Remove withered fronds in winter.

Propagate davallias by sowing spores or by dividing the fleshy stems. Select younger portions of the stems that show active growth and discard older pieces. Pin them to the surface of the potting mixture with bent wire and keep them constantly moist until new roots are firmly established, then water as directed above.

DAVALLIA See also *Microlepia* and *Scyphularia*

DENNSTAEDTIA

D. cicutaria, also called *D. rubiginosa* (common cup fern); *D. punctilobula* (hay-scented fern, boulder fern)

Both these ferns spread rapidly along creeping underground stems that quickly form dense mats. Some gardeners regard them as weeds because of their invasiveness, but this same habit also makes them useful as ground covers on steep slopes or in barren places where other plants are difficult to grow. Barriers of rockwork or metal lawn edging sunk into the ground help control their spread. Neither is grown as a house plant. The common cup fern is an evergreen fern with drooping 3- to 6-foot fronds. Both the fronds and their stout brown stalks are extremely hairy.

The hay-scented fern gets its common name, as might be expected, from the fact that its leaves, when crushed, give off the fragrance of new-mown hay. It has arching 1- to 3-foot fronds with hairy leaflets that grow 3 inches apart along the branching rhizomes.

HOW TO GROW. Outdoors, the common cup fern grows in gardens in Zones 7-10, while the hay-scented fern is one of the most adaptive garden ferns for use in Zones 3-8. Both are extremely tolerant of varying conditions of soil, sun and moisture. They grow best in moist, well-drained locations but will tolerate dry, open woods or swampy areas. They thrive in open shade but tolerate deep shade or even full sun if given sufficient moisture and humidity. In making a new bed, use a soil mix that is 1 part garden loam, 1 part builder's sand and 2 parts leaf mold or peat moss. A pH of 5.5 to 6.5 is ideal. The deciduous fronds of the hay-scented fern become dilapidated in late summer and brown early in fall, but do not remove them until spring, just before the new young growth, or fiddleheads, uncurl. To propagate either fern, cut rhizome mats apart in spring before new growth occurs and plant 2 feet apart. Both ferns can also be propagated from spores collected in late summer or fall.

DEER FERN See *Blechnum*
DELICATE MAIDENHAIR See *Adiantum*
DELTA MAIDENHAIR See *Adiantum*
DIAMOND MAIDENHAIR See *Adiantum*

DICKSONIA
D. antarctica (Tasmanian dicksonia, Tasmanian tree fern); *D. fibrosa* (woolly tree fern, fibrous dicksonia); *D. squarrosa* (slender tree fern)

Bearing broad crowns of fronds atop stout trunks, these tall tree ferns might be mistaken for palm trees. The trunks are actually frond stalks growing together in tight spirals; the stalks are covered with bristly hairs and matted aerial roots. Although dicksonias grow to great heights in the wild, young cultivated specimens 2 to 4 feet tall will not outgrow pots for several years. The Tasmanian dicksonia, which can grow 35 to 50 feet tall, has leathery, 6-foot fronds with leaflets that are crisscrossed by yellow veins. The slower-growing woolly tree fern seldom grows more than 20 feet tall; it has 8-foot fronds. The slender tree fern's horizontal 4-foot fronds form flat crowns on black trunks up to 20 feet tall.

HOW TO GROW. These tree ferns can be grown outdoors in Zones 9 and 10, particularly in cool, humid areas of California where the climate is tempered by the ocean, and night temperatures are lower than day. Choose sites with light to open shade that are protected from drying winds. The Tasmanian dicksonia will even stand full sun if the humidity is 60 to 80 per cent and the soil is constantly moist. Make new beds of 1 part garden loam, 1 part builder's sand and 2 parts leaf mold or peat moss. A pH of 6.0 to 7.0 is ideal.

Indoors, provide bright to very bright indirect or curtain-filtered sunlight (400 to 800 foot-candles). Day temperatures of 70° to 80°, cooling off to 50° to 60° at night are best, although these tree ferns will survive temperatures as low as 20° for short periods. Keep the soil constantly moist but not soggy, and provide 60 per cent or more humidity. Mist trunks during hot summer months; water less during winter. Repot only when root-bound. Use a mixture of equal parts packaged potting soil, builder's sand and peat moss or leaf mold; to each gallon pailful of this mixture, add 2 tablespoons of bone meal. Do not fertilize newly purchased or repotted plants for six months; feed established plants twice during the spring and summer growing season with fish emulsion diluted to half the strength recommended on the label.

Dicksonias are usually propagated from spores. The slender tree fern, and sometimes the Tasmanian dicksonia, occasionally form side shoots that grow from the base of the trunk at the soil line and can be severed to start new plants. When an offshoot has a trunk about an inch long and a frond spread of at least 10 inches, carefully remove the soil to expose the juncture of the shoot and the main plant. Cut the side shoot, taking care not to damage either the trunk of the parent plant or the threadlike roots of the new fern. Place the shoot in sterile potting mix in a 4-inch pot. Keep the soil moist but not soggy and provide 60 per cent humidity until roots have become well established.

DIPLAZIUM
D. esculentum, also called *Anisogonium esculentum, Athyrium esculentum* (vegetable fern); *D. proliferum*, also called *D. asperum, Anisogonium decussatum, Athyrium proliferum, Callipteris prolifera*

For climate zones and frost dates, see maps, pages 146-147.

TASMANIAN DICKSONIA
Dicksonia antarctica

VEGETABLE FERN
Diplazium esculentum

Diplazium proliferum

HACKSAW FERN
Doodia media

Although not classed as tree ferns, these two plants both can achieve 1- to 2-foot erect trunklike stems. Their arching whorls of 2- to 6-foot fronds have broad, wavy-edged leaflets. The vegetable fern, which is eaten in some tropical areas, is naturalized in Florida. *D. proliferum* bears tiny plantlets on the surface of its fronds.

HOW TO GROW. Grow these two ferns outdoors in Zones 9 and 10. Choose constantly moist, even slightly wet, sites in light shade. The vegetable fern will tolerate alternate sun and shade if it receives enough moisture. For a new bed, use a mixture of 1 part garden loam, 1 part builder's sand and 2 parts peat moss or leaf mold. A pH of 6.0 to 7.0 is best.

Indoors, provide bright indirect or curtain-filtered sunlight (400 foot-candles). The vegetable fern is able to tolerate very bright indirect light or a few hours of direct sunlight a day. They grow best when temperatures are 50° to 60° at night, 70° to 80° by day, and humidity is 60 per cent or, ideally, more. Repot root-bound specimens in a mix of equal parts packaged potting soil, builder's sand and leaf mold or peat moss; add 2 tablespoons of bone meal to each gallon of this mix. Do not fertilize newly purchased or repotted plants for six months; feed established plants twice a year during the spring and summer growing season using fish emulsion diluted to half the strength recommended on the label. Propagate either fern from spores; propagate *D. proliferum* by removing the plantlets from its fronds and placing them on moist potting soil until they root.

DOODIA

D. maxima, also called *D. blechnoides; D. media*, also called *D. lunulata, D. aspera* (both called hacksaw fern)

Hacksaw ferns send up tufts of rough-textured, 12- to 18-inch fronds from short, erect stems. The small leaflets with saw-toothed edges merge at the tips of the stiff fronds. Young foliage has an attractive red color. *D. media* grows more slowly and has smaller leaflets and narrower fronds than *D. maxima*. These ferns can be grown in window boxes or rock gardens in subtropical areas and indoors anywhere.

HOW TO GROW. Use hacksaw ferns outdoors in Zones 8-10 in open shade in locations that are moist to slightly dry. They will tolerate alternate sun and shade. These ferns do well in beds of 1 part garden loam, 1 part builder's sand and 2 parts peat moss or leaf mold. A pH of 5.5 to 6.5 is best.

Indoors, hacksaw ferns grow best in very bright indirect or curtain-filtered sunlight (800 foot-candles). Keep the soil moist, a little on the dry side, and water less in winter. Temperatures of 50° to 60° at night rising to 70° to 80° by day are ideal. Repot root-bound specimens in a mixture composed of equal parts packaged potting soil, builder's sand and peat moss or leaf mold; to each gallon pailful of this mixture, add 2 tablespoons of bone meal. Do not fertilize newly purchased or repotted plants for six months; feed established plants twice during the spring and summer growing season using fish emulsion diluted to half the minimum strength recommended on the label. Propagate by sowing spores or by dividing the thickened stem when repotting.

DORYOPTERIS

D. concolor, also called *Pellaea geraniifolia, Pteris geraniifolia; D. pedata palmata*, also called *Pteris palmata* (spear-leaved fern, hand fern)

These attractive tropical ferns have distinct hand-shaped fronds that somewhat resemble maple leaves. *D. concolor* is the larger of the two, with 6-inch fronds on wiry black stalks 15 inches long. The spear-leaved fern has two kinds of fronds. The broad, one-piece sterile leaves are carried on short stalks while the larger fertile fronds are on longer stalks and have narrower leaves cut into small leaflets. Both sterile and fertile foliage changes color as it matures, the leaves changing from light to dark green, the stalks from light green to brown to black. This fern is easy to propagate from the tiny buds that develop on both the sterile and fertile fronds at the junction of the leafy blade and the stalk.

HOW TO GROW. These ferns are not usually grown outdoors, although they might be tried in Zone 10 gardens.

Indoors, grow them in bright indirect or curtain-filtered sunlight (400 foot-candles). They do best when temperatures range from 60° to 70° at night, from 75° to 80° by day, and the humidity is 60 per cent or more. Keep the soil moist but not soggy. Repot root-bound specimens in a mixture of equal parts packaged potting soil, builder's sand and peat moss or leaf mold; add 2 tablespoons of bone meal to each gallon of this mixture. Do not fertilize newly purchased or repotted plants for six months; feed established specimens twice during the spring and summer growing season using fish emulsion diluted to half the strength recommended on the label.

Propagate either fern by sowing spores. The spear-leaved fern can also be propagated by removing plant buds from the fronds and pinning them to the surface of moist potting mix or by pegging a frond and its bulblets to moist soil, then severing the new plants from their parent after roots form.

DRYNARIA

D. quercifolia, also called *Polypodium quercifolium* (oak-leaf fern); *D. rigidula,* also called *Polypodium diversifolium, P. rigidulum*

These two ferns have distinct one-piece sterile leaves that resemble oak leaves. The short fronds overlap along fuzzy brown horizontal stems, or rhizomes, and collect humus for the plants, which grow on trees in their native Malaysia. Although the sterile leaves brown quickly, they remain attached to the rhizome a long time, unlike the deciduous fertile fronds, which wither and drop at the end of each growing season. The erect fertile fronds are as much as three times longer than sterile ones and are cut into tough leaflets. The oak leaf fern's 1-foot, wavy-edged sterile leaves surround 3-foot fertile fronds. *D. rigidula* is a slightly larger fern with fertile fronds that are erect when young but droop with age. The variety *D. rigidula whitei* has frilled leaflets so firm and leathery that they rattle when shaken.

HOW TO GROW. These ferns grow best as hanging basket plants outdoors in Zone 10 or indoors where temperatures are 60° to 70° at night, 75° to 80° by day, and humidity is 50 per cent. Outdoors they will grow in open shade or alternate sun and shade; indoors provide curtain-filtered or very bright indirect sunlight such as that reflected from light walls (800 foot-candles). Plant in a mixture of 1 part perlite or vermiculite to 1 part leaf mold or peat moss. Keep the mix moist, a little on the dry side, and fertilize once a month during the spring and summer growing season using fish emulsion diluted to half the strength recommended on the label.

Propagate from spores or by dividing the rhizomes when replanting in spring, just before new growth starts. Pin pieces of the horizontal stem that have growing tips to the surface of the soil; discard old, inactive parts.

DRYNARIA See also *Polypodium*

DRYOPTERIS

D. ampla, also called *Ctenitis sloanei* (American tree fern, Florida tree fern); *D. arguta* (coastal wood fern, California shield fern); *D. cristata* (crested shield fern); *D. decomposita,*

For climate zones and frost dates, see maps, pages 146-147.

SPEAR-LEAVED FERN
Doryopteris pedata palmata

OAK-LEAF FERN
Drynaria quercifolia

AMERICAN TREE FERN
Dryopteris ampla

COASTAL WOOD FERN
Dryopteris arguta

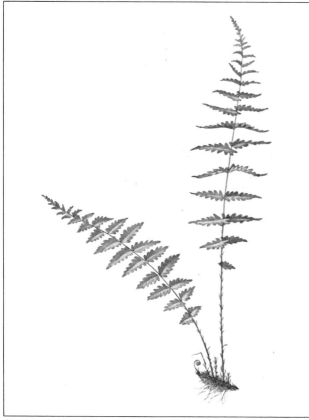

CRESTED SHIELD FERN
Dryopteris cristata

Dryopteris decomposita

also called *Lastreopsis microsora pentagularis, Ctenitis pentagularis; D. filix-mas* (male fern); *D. filix-mas cristata* (crested male fern); *D. goldiana* (Goldie's fern); *D. linnaeana,* also called *Gymnocarpium dryopteris* (oak fern); *D. noveboracensis,* also called *Thelypteris noveboracensis* (New York fern); *D. spinulosa intermedia,* also called *D. intermedia* (buckler fern, intermediate shield fern, fancy fern)

Plant classification specialists, known as taxonomists, differ greatly as to which ferns belong in the genus *Dryopteris,* but by any accepted classification system it includes a great many species—at least 150 ferns and as many as 1,000 according to some authorities. The ferns listed here are classified as *Dryopteris* by the Royal Horticultural Society in the second edition of its *Dictionary of Gardening.* However, since some reference works assign many to other genera, these are listed as "also called" to aid in locating plants.

Dryopteris species are distributed worldwide in both tropical and temperate regions. Most are medium-sized, coarse woodland ferns that adapt to many different growing conditions. Most have crowns of fronds arising from upright or short, creeping stems. New leaves develop underground one year and the crosiers rise and unfurl the following year. Sterile and fertile fronds look essentially the same. Dryopteris species have the deeply cut and finely subdivided leaflets that are commonly associated with ferns. Many hardy dryopteris are nearly evergreen, that is they will brown and wither after frost in Zones 3-6 but will stay green year round in parts of Zone 6 south to Zone 8.

The American tree fern is native to Florida. Its hairy stalks rise from an erect stem in a tight spiral, sometimes forming a small trunk 1½ feet tall. This trunk is topped by an arching canopy of fronds 3 feet in diameter.

The coastal wood fern, native from Washington to Southern California, forms tufts of 1- to 3-foot fronds along a tan, chaffy stem. The oblong, pointed fronds have paired, toothed-edged leaflets. The fern is nearly evergreen.

The narrow, leathery leaflets on the 1- to 3-foot fronds of the crested shield fern turn parallel to the ground, making each frond look like a miniature staircase. The shorter sterile fronds are evergreen, while the longer, narrower fertile fronds die back at the end of the growing season.

D. decomposita is a 1- to 2-foot nearly evergreen subtropical fern with broad fronds placed close together along their underground stem rather than in tufts or crowns. The toothed-edged leaflets have soft hairs on the undersides.

The male fern's long, triangular fronds are yellow-green when young, turning deep green as they mature. The 2- to 4-foot leathery fertile fronds are deciduous and die after freezing, while sterile ones are nearly evergreen. Commercial collectors have harvested entire colonies of this popular fern, almost eliminating it from the wild in some areas; since it is now becoming rare, it should not be dug from forests.

The crested male fern, developed by English horticulturists, resembles the male fern except that the tips of the fronds and of the leaflets fork into finger-like divisions.

Goldie's fern is the largest dryopteris species. Massive, rugged fronds 4 feet long and 1½ feet wide are usual, but plants can grow to 5 feet under ideal conditions. The foliage is deciduous. Leathery, 7- to 8-inch leaflets, set closer together on scaly stalks, end in a sharp point. The heavily scaled crosiers form very dense crowns.

The oak fern is more delicate. The light green fronds are composed of three triangular, stalked leaflets that are arranged somewhat like those of a three-leaf clover. The 4- to 11-inch deciduous foliage is commonly as broad as it is long.

The New York fern's narrow 1- to 2-foot fronds have

For climate zones and frost dates, see maps, pages 146-147.

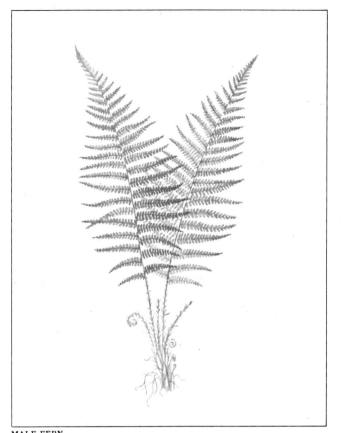

MALE FERN
Dryopteris filix-mas

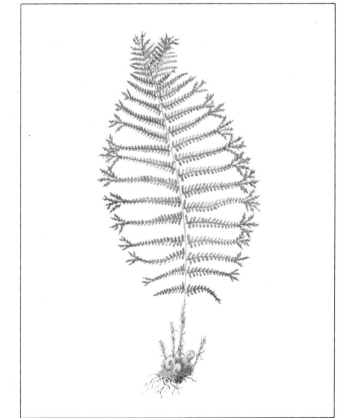

CRESTED MALE FERN
Dryopteris filix-mas cristata

GOLDIE'S FERN
Dryopteris goldiana

OAK FERN
Dryopteris linnaeana

NEW YORK FERN
Dryopteris noveboracensis

BUCKLER FERN
Dryopteris spinulosa intermedia

tapering leaflets, pointed at both their tips and bases but so broad in the middle that their edges overlap. The deciduous fronds of this fern have coarse white bristles along their edges and are hairy underneath.

The 1- to 3-foot buckler fern is commonly used in commercial flower arrangements. The thin-textured fronds are picked during the summer, then held in cold storage for use by florists in the winter. The stalks are twice the length of the finely cut, evergreen foliage.

HOW TO GROW. Dryopteris species are known for their ease of cultivation. The 10 ferns in this list offer a choice for woodland gardens with varying degrees of light and moisture in almost every climate zone. Gardeners in Zones 3-8 can choose the crested shield fern, the male fern, the crested male fern, Goldie's fern, the oak fern, the New York or the buckler fern for their woodland plantings. The coastal wood fern is less hardy, therefore it and *D. decomposita* may be grown in Zones 7-10, the American tree fern in Zone 10.

Outdoor sites with open shade are good locations for the American tree fern, *D. decomposita*, Goldie's fern and the New York fern. The crested shield fern and the buckler fern grow best in light shade. The coastal wood fern will grow in light or deep shade. Give the male fern, crested male fern and oak fern deep shade.

Most dryopteris thrive in soils that are constantly moist but not soggy. The coastal wood fern, however, grows best in well-drained, slightly dry soil, and the crested shield fern thrives in boggy, wet soil. In preparing new beds, use a mixture of 1 part garden loam, 1 part builder's sand and 2 parts peat moss or leaf mold. A pH of 5.5 to 6.5 is best for all except the American tree fern which is suited to a pH of 7.0 to 8.0. To raise the pH, add approximately 2 tablespoons of ground limestone per cubic foot of soil.

Hardy dryopteris species do not grow well indoors or in pots. Of the species listed here, the American tree fern and *D. decomposita* are the best choices for indoor pot culture. Indoors, give them curtain-filtered or bright to very bright indirect sunlight, such as that reflected from light walls (400 to 800 foot-candles). Temperatures of 50° to 60° at night, 70° to 80° by day, and 60 per cent humidity are ideal. Keep the soil moist but not soggy, and use a mixture of equal parts packaged potting soil, leaf mold or peat moss, and builder's sand. Add 2 tablespoons of bone meal to each gallon of mix for either fern; also add a tablespoon of ground limestone to each gallon for the American tree fern. Propagate all these ferns by sowing spores or dividing their crowns or stems.

DUCKWEED FERN See *Azolla*
DUFF'S SWORD FERN See *Nephrolepis*
DUTCH RUSH See *Equisetum*

E

EAST INDIAN HOLLY FERN See *Polystichum*
EASTERN CHAIN FERN See *Woodwardia*
EBONY SPLEENWORT See *Asplenium*
ELEPHANT'S-EAR FERN See *Platycerium*

EQUISETUM
E. hyemale, also spelled *E. hiemale* (scouring rush, Dutch rush); *E. scorpiodes,* also called *E. scirpoides* (dwarf scouring rush); *E. variegatum* (variegated scouring rush) (all called horsetails)

Horsetails are evergreen, reedy plants with hollow, jointed stems that prosper in an outdoor, waterside location. Their ancestry can be traced back to the prehistoric plants of the Carboniferous age that formed large forests and eventually

SCOURING RUSH
Equisetum hyemale

For climate zones and frost dates, see maps, pages 146-147.

became the coal deposits of today. Tiny scalelike leaves grow at the stem joints and fertile stems are tipped with a conical structure in summer that produces the spores. Their underground stems spread widely and rapidly, making them difficult to eradicate once established. The silica in their stems makes them useful for polishing and scrubbing.

The scouring rush grows to 4 feet while the dwarf scouring rush is only 6 inches tall. The dwarf species, the smallest known horsetail, has twisting, twining stems that form tangled mats. The tiny leaves of the 15-inch variegated scouring rush are banded black and white.

HOW TO GROW. Horsetails grow best outdoors in Zones 3-8. Plant them in full sun in constantly moist to wet soil with a pH of 6.0 to 7.0. In new garden beds, use a mixture of 1 part garden loam, 1 part builder's sand and 2 parts leaf mold or peat moss. To control their spreading habit, place clumps in pots and sink the pots in the garden.

While horsetails do not make good house plants, the variegated scouring rush is sometimes grown indoors in pots. Provide direct sun or very bright indirect or curtain-filtered sunlight (800 foot-candles). Temperatures of 45° to 55° at night, 65° to 75° by day and 60 per cent humidity are ideal. Plant in a mixture of equal parts packaged potting soil, builder's sand and leaf mold or peat moss; add 2 tablespoons of bone meal per gallon of mix. Fertilize twice during the spring and summer growing season with fish emulsion diluted to half the strength recommended on the label. Stand the pot in a saucer of water to keep the soil wet. Propagate by division or from spores. The green spores that mature in summer must be sown within a few days or they will not grow.

F

FANCY FERN See *Dryopteris*
FELT FERN, JAPANESE See *Cyclophorus*
FIBROUS DICKSONIA See *Dicksonia*
FIJI DAVALLIA See *Davallia*
FILMY FERN See *Hymenophyllum* and *Trichomanes*
FISHTAIL SWORD FERN See *Nephrolepis*
FIVE-FINGER FERN See *Adiantum*
FLOATING STAGHORN FERN See *Ceratopteris*
FLORIDA TREE FERN See *Dryopteris*
FLOWERING FERN See *Anemia*
FLUFFY RUFFLES See *Nephrolepis*
FRAGILE BLADDER FERN See *Cystopteris*

G

GIANT CHAIN FERN See *Woodwardia*
GIANT FERN See *Acrostichum*
GLADE FERN See *Athyrium*
GOLDBACK FERN See *Pityrogramma*
GOLDEN POLYPODY See *Polypodium*
GOLD FERN See *Pityrogramma*
GOLDIE'S FERN See *Dryopteris*
GONIOPHLEBIUM See *Polypodium*
GRAPE FERN See *Botrychium*
GREEN CLIFF BRAKE See *Pellaea*
GYMNOCARPIUM See *Dryopteris*

H

HACKSAW FERN See *Doodia*
HAIRY LIP FERN See *Cheilanthes*
HAMMOCK FERN See *Blechnum*
HAND FERN See *Doryopteris*
HAPU See *Cibotium*
HARTFORD FERN See *Lygodium*
HART'S-TONGUE FERN See *Phyllitis*

Hemionitis arifolia

HAWAIIAN TREE FERN See *Cibotium*
HAY-SCENTED FERN See *Dennstaedtia*

HEMIONITIS
H. arifolia; H. palmata (strawberry fern)

These low-growing tropical ferns, which are well suited to terrariums, have broad-leaved fronds that resemble some foliage house plants more than they do the leafy fern species most gardeners are familiar with. *H. arifolia* has leathery, arrowhead-shaped foliage that is smooth and mottled with cream-colored markings on the leaves of young plants. The 5-inch fertile leaves are carried on black stalks up to 12 inches long; barren leaves are the same size but on shorter stalks. The foliage of the strawberry fern is shaped like the palm of a hand. The edges of the five broad lobes or fingers are irregularly scalloped. Both upper and lower surfaces of the 5- to 6-inch fronds are covered with fine short hairs. Stalks of the stiff fertile leaves are up to 6 inches long, sterile ones are shorter. The strawberry fern produces tiny plantlets at its base and at the junction of the stalk and frond.

HOW TO GROW. Not usually grown outdoors, these two ferns grow best in indoor pots or terrariums. They thrive in bright indirect or curtain-filtered sunlight (400 foot-candles) with temperatures of 60° to 70° at night, 75° to 80° by day, and humidity of 60 per cent or more. Keep the soil moist, neither on the wet nor dry side. Repot root-bound specimens in a mixture of equal parts packaged potting soil, builder's sand and peat moss or leaf mold; add 2 tablespoons of bone meal to each gallon of this mixture. Do not fertilize newly purchased or repotted plants for six months; feed established plants twice during the spring and summer growing season using fish emulsion diluted to half the strength recommended on the label. Propagate either fern from spores or by dividing the plants when repotting. The strawberry fern can also be propagated by removing the plantlets and pinning them to the surface of moist potting mix until they root.

HOLLY FERN See *Cyrtomium*
HOLLY FERN, EAST INDIAN See *Polystichum*
HOLLY FERN, JAPANESE See *Cyrtomium*
HOLLY FERN, TSUSSIMA See *Polystichum*

HUMATA
H. tyermannii (bear's-foot fern)

The slow-growing bear's-foot fern, one of the most commonly grown house ferns, can be planted in a pot, terrarium or hanging basket. The leathery triangular fronds, up to 9 inches long, are spaced up to 3 inches apart along a branching horizontal stem covered with shiny white scales. The furry appearance of these stems gives the fern its common name. New fronds are slightly red in contrast to the green of older fronds and the white of the "feet." The bear's-foot fern is deciduous, but in a warm, humid climate where it is used as a ground cover or rock garden plant, it may not shed older fronds until after new ones have appeared. *Humata* species are similar to *Davallia*, and some ferns sold as bear's-foot ferns may be species of *Davallia*.

HOW TO GROW. The bear's-foot fern is grown outdoors in Zones 9 and 10. Choose moist to slightly dry sites in light shade or alternate sun and shade. In preparing a bed, use a mixture of 1 part garden loam, 1 part builder's sand and 2 parts peat moss or leaf mold. A pH of 6.0 to 7.0 is ideal.

Indoors, this fern grows best in curtain-filtered or bright to very bright indirect sunlight such as that reflected from light walls (400 to 800 foot-candles). Temperatures of 50° to 60° at night, 70° to 80° by day and 50 per cent humidity are

STRAWBERRY FERN
Hemionitis palmata

BEAR'S-FOOT FERN
Humata tyermannii

For climate zones and frost dates, see maps, pages 146-147.

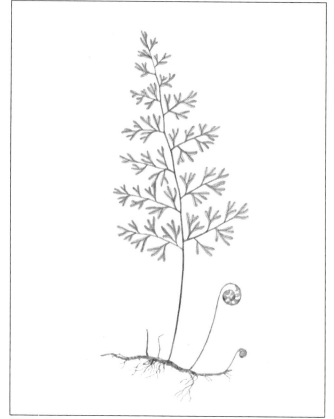

FILMY FERN
Hymenophyllum demissum

BRAMBLE FERN
Hypolepis repens

best. Keep the soil moist but allow it to dry slightly between waterings. Browning of the white scales on the stems indicates overwatering. In a pot or terrarium, use equal parts packaged potting soil, builder's sand and peat moss or leaf mold and add 2 tablespoons of bone meal per gallon of mix; do not feed newly purchased or repotted plants for six months; feed established plants twice during the spring and summer growing season using fish emulsion diluted to half the strength recommended on the label. In hanging baskets, use a mixture of 1 part perlite or vermiculite to 1 part leaf mold or peat moss; fertilize baskets once a month with fish emulsion used half strength. The bear's-foot fern can remain in a pot or basket several years. Its furry stems will grow over one another without any harm to the plant.

Propagate by spores or by dividing the furry stems when repotting, pinning pieces showing active growth to the surface of moist potting mix.

HYMENOPHYLLUM
H. demissum, also called *Mecodium demissum* (filmy fern)

The 1- to 9-inch-high, pale green filmy fern spaces delicate, almost translucent fronds only one cell thick along a threadlike horizontal stem. In their natural environment, filmy ferns are found in deep shade, clinging to trees and rocks where water percolating through the soil keeps them constantly moist. They can be grown in terrariums or glass domes, though they are difficult subjects.

HOW TO GROW. Filmy ferns have exacting growing requirements. Provide a very low level of indirect sunlight, such as that in a north window (150 foot-candles). Avoid any direct sun. Night temperatures of 50° to 60° and day temperatures of 70° to 80° are ideal. This fern needs 100 per cent humidity. To provide the necessary humidity, mist filmy ferns several times a week with salt-free water. Water freely during the spring and summer growing season, less in winter. Plant the ferns on tree fern fiber or anchor the threadlike stems to rocks with nylon fish line. Fertilize once a year during the growing season. While a constantly moist atmosphere is necessary, terrariums and domes should be ventilated for a few minutes each day to provide the air circulation essential to avoid overheating. Filmy ferns are occasionally grown in fern cases specially constructed so that they can be air conditioned and humidified automatically. They are usually propagated by division of the thin stems.

HYPOLEPIS
H. punctata; H. repens (bramble fern)

The large triangular fronds of these ferns, as much as 3 or 4 feet long and 1½ feet broad, rise from a ropy, hairy underground stem that spreads so rapidly that it soon forces less robust ferns out of the garden. The fine foliage is divided into soft leaflets with scalloped edges. *H. punctata*'s papery fronds have purple stalks. The bramble fern's delicate appearance is deceiving, for its long brown stalks and the rib down the center of each frond are covered with prickly spines. These ferns are easy to grow as ground covers or foundation plantings in subtropical areas.

HOW TO GROW. These ferns can be grown outdoors in Zone 10, especially in marshy or damp areas with light shade. In preparing a new bed, use a mixture of 1 part garden loam, 1 part builder's sand and 2 parts leaf mold or peat moss. They tolerate acid or neutral soils, with a pH from 5.5 to 7.0.

Indoors, these ferns can be used as pot plants where night temperatures are 50° to 60°, day temperatures are 70° to 80°, and the humidity is 60 per cent or more. Give them bright indirect or curtained-filtered sunlight (400 foot-candles) and keep the soil constantly moist but not soggy. Plant in a mixture of equal parts packaged potting soil, builder's sand and peat moss or leaf mold; add 2 tablespoons of bone meal to each gallon of this mixture. Do not fertilize newly purchased or repotted plants for six months; feed established plants twice during the spring and summer growing season using fish emulsion diluted to half the strength recommended on the label. Propagate by dividing the underground stems in spring or from spores at any time.

I

INDIAN'S DREAM See *Pellaea*
INTERMEDIATE SHIELD FERN See *Dryopteris*
INTERRUPTED FERN See *Osmunda*

J

JAPANESE CLAW FERN See *Onychium*
JAPANESE CLIMBING FERN See *Lygodium*
JAPANESE FELT FERN See *Cyclophorus*
JAPANESE HOLLY FERN See *Cyrtomium*
JAPANESE PAINTED FERN See *Athyrium*
JAVA STAGHORN FERN See *Platycerium*
JOINTED POLYPODY See *Polypodium*

K

KILLARNEY FERN See *Trichomanes*

L

LACE FERN See *Cheilanthes*
LACY LEAF GRAPE FERN See *Botrychium*
LADY FERN See *Athyrium*
LAMB, SCYTHIAN See *Cibotium*
LASTREA See *Polystichum*
LASTREOPSIS See *Dryopteris*
LEATHER FERN See *Acrostichum* and *Polystichum*
LEATHER GRAPE FERN See *Botrychium*
LEATHERLEAF See *Polypodium*
LEATHERY POLYPODY See *Polypodium*

LEMMAPHYLLUM
L. microphyllum

This tiny, low-growing plant does not look like a fern. The smooth-edged, one-piece, fleshy fronds are closely spaced on a thin, creeping stem that will twine like a vine up moist surfaces. The fertile spore-bearing fronds are extremely narrow, the sterile ones nearly oval. *L. microphyllum* is seldom grown in the garden, even in warmer zones, but it can be used indoors as a pot or terrarium plant; it grows very slowly.

HOW TO GROW. *L. microphyllum* needs bright indirect or curtain-filtered sunlight (400 foot-candles), temperatures of 50° to 60° at night, 70° to 80° by day, and 60 per cent humidity. Keep it moist but never soggy in a mixture of 1 part leaf mold or peat moss, 1 part builder's sand and 2 parts perlite or vermiculite; add 2 tablespoons of bone meal to each gallon of this mix. Do not fertilize newly purchased or repotted plants for six months; feed established ferns twice during the spring and summer growing season using fish emulsion diluted to half the strength recommended on the label. *L. microphyllum* can also be grown on tree fern or osmunda fiber; fertilize plants on these soilless media once a month. Propagate from spores or stem divisions.

LICORICE FERN See *Polypodium*
LITTLE GRAY POLYPODY See *Polypodium*
LIP FERN See *Cheilanthes*
LORINSERIA See *Woodwardia*

Lemmaphyllum microphyllum

For climate zones and frost dates, see maps, pages 146-147.

JAPANESE CLIMBING FERN
Lygodium japonicum

HARTFORD FERN
Lygodium palmatum

LYGODIUM

L. japonicum, also called *L. scandens, Ophioglossum japonicum* (Japanese climbing fern); *L. palmatum* (Hartford fern, climbing fern)

These two climbing ferns send out thin, wiry twining leaf stalks up to 15 feet long that coil around any nearby plants or supports. The Japanese climbing fern has green papery triangular leaflets up to 8 inches long and equally broad. The sterile and fertile forked fronds are similar in shape but sterile leaflets are broader. The fronds die back each year and new ones grow each spring. It is often used as a ground cover or as a trellis plant outdoors. Indoors, the Japanese climbing fern makes an excellent house plant for pots or hanging baskets. It can also be grown on strings in a window as a leafy curtain.

The Hartford fern was the first fern to be protected by legislation. In 1869 the Connecticut legislature passed a conservation law to prevent its extermination by collectors who picked plants from the wild for home decoration. It has evergreen hand-shaped and sterile leaflets, 2 inches long and wide. The very narrow forked fertile leaflets clustered at the tip are deciduous.

HOW TO GROW. The Japanese climbing fern grows best outdoors in Zones 7-10 in light shade or alternate sun and shade. Plant it in a moist but not soggy location. In preparing a new bed, use 1 part garden loam, 1 part builder's sand and 2 parts peat moss or leaf mold. A pH of 5.5 to 6.5 is ideal.

Although the Hartford fern occurs naturally in Zones 5-8 from Massachusetts south to Georgia, it is extremely difficult to transplant to the garden. It needs light to deep shade and moist, undisturbed, strongly acid soil—pH of 5.0 or less—that is deficient in nutrients. Culture outdoors can be attempted in a mixture of builder's sand and sphagnum moss. Collect and use rain water for this fern, as any lime or traces of metals that might be introduced by plumbing pipes may kill it. This plant is almost impossible to grow indoors.

When the Japanese climbing fern is grown indoors, give it bright to very bright indirect or curtain-filtered sunlight (400 to 800 foot-candles). Temperatures of 50° to 60° at night, 70° to 80° by day, and 60 per cent humidity are ideal. Keep the soil moist but not wet. In pots, use a mixture of equal parts packaged potting soil, builder's sand and leaf mold or peat moss; add 2 tablespoons of bone meal per gallon of mix. Provide a support for the fern to climb. Remove old fronds in spring before new ones emerge and become tangled with them. Do not fertilize newly purchased or repotted plants for six months; feed established plants twice during the spring and summer growing season using fish emulsion diluted to half the strength recommended on the label. In hanging baskets, use a mixture of 1 part perlite or vermiculite to 1 part leaf mold or peat moss and fertilize the basket once a month with fish emulsion used half strength.

Propagate either of these climbing ferns from spores. The Japanese climbing fern can also be divided in spring before it puts out new growth.

M

MAIDENHAIR FERN See *Adiantum*
MAIDENHAIR SPLEENWORT See *Asplenium*
MALE FERN See *Dryopteris*
MAMAKU See *Cyathea*

MARSILEA

M. quadrifolia (water clover fern, pepperwort, water shamrock)

In still, fresh water locations, this 3- to 8-inch aquatic plant anchors its wiry rootstocks in the mud and floats its leaflets—which resemble four-leaf clovers—on or just below the surface of the water. The peppercorn-sized spore cases are borne on separate, short stalks at the base of leaf stalks. In shallower water, where stouter stems hold the leaflets above the surface of the water, opposing leaflets fold up at night. The water clover spreads rapidly and can easily become a pest in the garden pond.

HOW TO GROW. Grow water clover outdoors in ponds or along the sides of quiet brooks in Zones 4-8. It grows best in extremely wet locations in open shade or full sun. When making new outdoor beds, use a soil mix consisting of approximately 1 part garden loam, 1 part builder's sand and 2 parts leaf mold or peat moss. A pH of 5.5 to 6.5 is best.

Indoors, plant the water clover in aquariums, wet terrariums or shallow pots where the plants receive direct sun or very bright indirect light such as that reflected from light walls (800 foot-candles or more). Temperatures of 45° to 55° at night, 65° to 75° by day and 60 per cent or more humidity are ideal. In terrariums or shallow pots use a mixture of equal parts packaged potting soil, leaf mold or peat moss, and builder's sand; add 2 tablespoons of bone meal to each gallon of this mixture. Stand pots in saucers of water to keep the soil wet. Do not fertilize newly purchased or repotted plants for six months; feed established plants twice during the spring and summer growing season using fish-emulsion fertilizer diluted to half the strength recommended on the label. Water clover can be propagated by sowing spores or dividing the rootstock.

MATTEUCCIA

M. struthiopteris, also called *M. pensylvanica, M. struthiopteris pensylvanica, Pteretis nodulosa* (ostrich fern)

In the wild, the bold, plumy fronds of the ostrich fern can grow to 10 feet, making it one of the largest American ferns. In the garden, however, it is usually smaller, with vase-shaped clusters of 3- to 5-foot fronds rising from heavy crowns and its bold shape makes it a good accent for woodland gardens where there is enough space for it. These crowns are spaced along a spreading network of ropy underground runners, creating a dense mat of roots and runners that will hold soil along stream banks. The shiny, dark green balls of the crosiers are among the last to appear in the spring. The leathery, blunt sterile fronds unfurl first and surround the hard, woody fertile fronds, which appear in late summer. The bronze fertile fronds, about half the height of the sterile ones, have compact heads of extremely narrow leaflets. The sterile leaves become ragged at the end of the summer and brown early in the fall. Although the fertile fronds also brown, they remain erect through the winter. This fern grows robustly and has a tendency to spread. The ostrich fern is not usually grown indoors, although young plants started from spores can be grown in pots until they are large enough to transplant outdoors.

HOW TO GROW. The ostrich fern grows in Zones 3-8 in moist to wet locations. It does best in light shade; however, it will grow in deep shade and it will also tolerate full sun if it has enough moisture. In preparing a new bed, use 1 part garden loam, 1 part builder's sand and 2 parts leaf mold or peat moss. A pH of 5.5 to 6.5 is ideal. Propagate at any time by sowing spores or in early spring by division of the crown-forming underground stems. Set divisions 2 to 3 feet apart.

MAURITIUS MOTHER FERN See *Asplenium*
MECODIUM See *Hymenophyllum*
MEXICAN TREE FERN See *Cibotium*

For climate zones and frost dates, see maps, pages 146-147.

WATER CLOVER FERN
Marsilea quadrifolia

OSTRICH FERN
Matteuccia struthiopteris

Microlepia platyphylla

Microlepia strigosa

MICROLEPIA

M. platyphylla, also called *Davallia lonchitidea*, *D. platyphylla*; *M. speluncae*, also called *Davallia polypodioides*; *M. strigosa*, also called *Davallia khasyana*

Microlepias are vigorous and graceful ferns of medium to large size that make attractive background plantings in subtropical woodland gardens. The broad, hairy fronds become smooth as they mature. The stout, hairy rootstock branches as it grows, forming compact clumps. Unlike most ferns, its frond stalks are continuous with the rootstock, rather than jointed where the stalk and rootstock meet.

The broad, coarse fronds of *M. platyphylla* grow 6 to 10 feet tall in the garden. Grown in the shade, its fronds are blue-green; in sunny positions they become pale green. This fern is nearly evergreen, but it has a long dormant period in fall and winter. *M. speluncae* grows 3 to 6 feet tall and has papery, spear-shaped leaflets up to a foot long. It is evergreen. *M. strigosa*, 3 feet tall, has arching, triangular fronds up to a foot wide; it also is evergreen.

While *M. strigosa* is sometimes used as a pot plant, *M. platyphylla* and *M. speluncae* are seldom seen indoors because of their large size. However, young plants can be grown in pots until they are large enough to be transplanted to outdoor locations.

HOW TO GROW. With the exception of *M. speluncae*, these rapid-growing microlepias can be grown outdoors in Zones 7-10; *M. speluncae* grows in Zone 10. *M. platyphylla* and *M. speluncae* grow best in light shade, while *M. strigosa* thrives in open shade. Plant these ferns in moist to slightly dry soil. In preparing a new bed, use a mixture of 1 part garden loam, 1 part builder's sand and 2 parts leaf mold or peat moss. A pH of 5.5 to 6.5 is ideal.

Indoors, grow them in bright to very bright indirect or curtain-filtered sunlight (400 to 800 foot-candles). Temperatures of 50° to 60° at night, 70° to 80° by day and 60 per cent humidity are best. Keep the soil moist, allowing it to dry slightly between waterings. Use a potting mix of equal parts packaged potting soil, builder's sand and leaf mold or peat moss; add 2 tablespoons of bone meal per gallon of mix. Do not feed newly purchased or repotted plants for six months; feed established plants twice during the spring and summer growing season using fish emulsion diluted to half the strength recommended on the label.

These ferns grow so rapidly that clumps triple in size in one growing season. Divide them regularly and place the divisions 2 feet apart. Be sure each division has a growing tip where new fronds are developing. Microlepias can also be propagated from spores sown on moist potting mix.

MONKEY'S-PAW FERN See *Scyphularia*
MOSQUITO FERN See *Azolla*
MOTHER FERN See *Asplenium*
MOTHER SPLEENWORT See *Asplenium*
MOUNTAIN WOODSIA See *Woodsia*

N

NARROW-LEAVED CHAIN FERN See *Woodwardia*
NARROW-LEAVED STRAP FERN See *Polypodium*

NEPHROLEPIS

N. biserrata furcans (fishtail sword fern); *N. cordifolia duffii* (Duff's sword fern); *N. exaltata bostoniensis compacta*; *N. exaltata* 'Fluffy Ruffles'; *N. exaltata* 'Mini-Ruffle'; *N. exaltata norwoodii* (Norwood sword fern)

For many plant fanciers, the word "fern" calls forth an image of the Boston fern or one of its many cultivars. Known botanically as *N. exaltata bostoniensis*, the familiar Boston fern is a mutant of the sword fern, *N. exaltata*. This famous mutant, a plant that has undergone a chance genetic change and has characteristics different from those of its parent, not only reproduces itself but also has parented numerous mutations of its own. The Boston fern with broader, more arching fronds and its mutant cultivated varieties with their ruffled, crested and fluffy appearance have now eclipsed the original sword fern in popularity. Attractive foliage is not the only characteristic that endears the Boston fern and its offspring to fern growers. These plants are extremely sturdy, almost indestructible house plants—a characteristic common to many sword fern species.

The sword ferns in this list offer a choice of sizes and forms. They are often grown as border or rock-garden plants outdoors, as well as indoor pot plants. Their arching fronds make them dramatic plants to display on pedestals or in hanging baskets. The fishtail sword fern has drooping fronds up to 4½ feet long and a foot wide. The leaflets fork at their tips, hence the name fishtail. Duff's sword fern has extremely narrow, erect foliage. The 2-foot fronds are only ½ inch wide and the tiny leaflets are forked or crested at their tips. *Compacta* is the commonly sold dwarf form of the Boston fern, growing only half the usual 3-foot size of the Boston fern. The leaves of Fluffy Ruffles are divided so many times into such fine leaflets and are crowded so tightly together that its fronds look like explosions of green lace. The dense foliage of this Boston fern cultivar is stiff when young, but arches gracefully as it reaches its full 1½- to 2-foot length. Mini-Ruffle resembles it but only grows to half the size. The Norwood sword fern is another Boston fern offspring with finely divided foliage, but the leaves are spaced farther apart than those of Fluffy Ruffles. The 1½-foot fronds resemble ladders with puffy rungs.

HOW TO GROW. Sword ferns can be grown outdoors in Zone 10 in deep to open shade. They do best in well-drained soils that are moist but slightly on the dry side. In preparing a new bed, use a mixture that is 1 part garden loam, 1 part builder's sand and 2 parts leaf mold or peat moss. A pH of 6.0 to 7.0 is ideal.

Indoors, sword ferns will tolerate low levels of indirect or curtain-filtered sunlight such as that in the shadowless light of a north window and they will thrive in very bright indirect light such as that reflected from light walls (150 to 800 foot-candles). Temperatures of 60° to 70° at night, 75° to 80° by day, and humidity from 50 to 60 per cent are ideal. Keep them moist but allow the soil to dry slightly between waterings. In pots, use a mixture of 1 part peat moss or leaf mold, 1 part builder's sand and 2 parts perlite or vermiculite; add 2 tablespoons of bone meal per gallon of mix. For a lighter soil in hanging baskets, use a mixture of 1 part leaf mold or peat moss and 1 part perlite or vermiculite. Both of these mixes are low in nutrients, so the plants should be fertilized once a month during the spring and summer growing season using fish emulsion fertilizer diluted to half the strength recommended on the label.

Sword ferns do best when their roots fill the pot but are not crowded. When repotting, use a pot only one size larger. Trim older fronds as they yellow. Tuck the long, slender hairy stems or stolons that these ferns produce into the pot to hide them or cut them off.

All of these ferns can be propagated by pegging the stolons to the surface of moist potting mix until they take root, then cutting them from the parent plant. Sword ferns can also be propagated by dividing their crowns or stems when repotting. Many Boston fern cultivars are sterile and produce no

FISHTAIL SWORD FERN
Nephrolepis biserrata furcans

For climate zones and frost dates, see maps, pages 146-147.

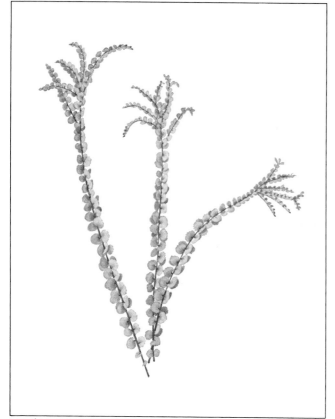

DUFF'S SWORD FERN
Nephrolepis cordifolia duffii

FLUFFY RUFFLES
Nephrolepis exaltata 'Fluffy Ruffles'

NORWOOD SWORD FERN
Nephrolepis exaltata norwoodii

SENSITIVE FERN
Onoclea sensibilis

spores. Other sword ferns produce spores, and this method of propagating is used for some of the rarer plants in this genus of about 30 species.

NET-VEINED CHAIN FERN See *Woodwardia*
NEW YORK FERN See *Dryopteris*
NEW ZEALAND CLIFF BRAKE See *Pellaea*
NIPHOBOLUS See *Cyclophorus*
NORTHERN MAIDENHAIR See *Adiantum*
NORWOOD SWORD FERN See *Nephrolepis*

O

OAK FERN See *Dryopteris*
OAK-LEAF FERN See *Drynaria*

ONOCLEA

O. sensibilis (sensitive fern, bead fern)

When the coarse, thin fronds of this 2- to 4-foot fern are picked, they wilt rapidly, and they are the first fronds to be killed by autumn frosts. These two folk observations lead to its common name. In spring, red croisers or new growth unfurl into the large sterile fronds with broad scalloped or coarsely toothed leaflets. The narrow fertile fronds resembling tightly rolled beads rise in late summer. The sterile fronds are deciduous and wither after frost. The fertile stalks turn from green to brown as they mature and remain standing through the winter. The beads crack open to shed their spores the following spring. The sensitive fern's underground stem spreads rapidly to form extensive mats, making it useful as a ground cover. Because of its size and coarseness, this fern is not used as a house plant.

HOW TO GROW. The sensitive fern thrives in wet, boggy sites in Zones 3-8, and will sometimes grow in Zone 9. Open shade is best, but it will tolerate direct sun if there is enough moisture. In preparing new beds, use a mixture of 1 part garden loam, 1 part builder's sand and 2 parts leaf mold or peat moss. A pH of 6.0 to 7.0 is ideal.

Propagate the sensitive fern by collecting green spores in spring and sowing them immediately on damp potting mix. Spores that are not fresh germinate poorly. The fern's extensive stem system can also be cut into sections and the divisions planted 2 to 3 feet apart.

ONYCHIUM

O. japonicum, also called *O. capense* (Japanese claw fern, carrot fern)

Narrow pointed leaflets resembling birds' claws on the fronds of the Japanese claw fern give them the same feathery, lacy appearance that carrot tops have. The 12-inch-long, 6-inch-wide evergreen fronds are carried on stalks a foot high rising from a shallow underground stem. The fronds make long-lasting additions to floral bouquets.

HOW TO GROW. Grow the Japanese claw fern outdoors in light shade in Zones 7-10 where the soil is moist but not soggy. To prepare a new bed, use a mixture of 1 part garden loam, 1 part builder's sand and 2 parts leaf mold or peat moss. A pH of 5.5 to 6.5 is best.

Indoors, provide very bright indirect or curtain-filtered sunlight such as that reflected from light walls (800 foot-candles). This fern grows best when temperatures are 50° to 60° by night, 70° to 80° by day, and the humidity is 60 per cent. Keep the soil constantly moist but not wet, and plant the fern in a mixture of equal parts packaged potting soil, builder's sand and leaf mold or peat moss; add 2 tablespoons of bone meal per gallon of mix. Do not fertilize newly purchased or repotted plants for six months; feed established

JAPANESE CLAW FERN
Onychium japonicum

For climate zones and frost dates, see maps, pages 146-147.

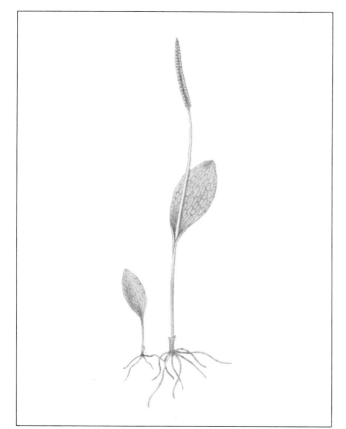

NORTHERN ADDER'S-TONGUE FERN
Ophioglossum vulgatum

CINNAMON FERN
Osmunda cinnamomea

plants twice during the spring and summer growing season using fish emulsion diluted to half the strength recommended on the label. Propagate the Japanese claw fern by sowing spores or dividing the clumps of stems when repotting.

ONYCHIUM See also *Pellaea*

OPHIOGLOSSUM

O. petiolatum (southern adder's-tongue fern); *O. vulgatum* (northern adder's-tongue fern)

Watch closely for the tiny adder's-tongue fern in the grass along wooded paths or open pastures, on bog borders or on shaded sandstone ledges. Each spring a solitary round shoot rises straight up 2 to 4 inches, then unfolds into a 3- to 6-inch oval sterile leaf. The tongue, which grows 1 to 3 inches above the base of this smooth, leathery leaf, is the fern's flat fertile spike, embedded with two vertical rows of spore cases. These cases split open in early summer to free the ripe yellow spores, and the leaf withers by midsummer. The fern's fleshy roots spread 2 inches below the soil surface. Buds that form along these roots can create a whole colony from one plant. The adder's-tongue fern is grown outdoors in rock or wild gardens. The southern species shares its curious form with the northern counterpart but is easier to grow indoors in a pot or terrarium.

HOW TO GROW. The adder's-tongue fern grows best in open shade in moist, well-drained soils. Plant it outdoors in Zones 7-10 in 1 part garden loam, 1 part builder's sand and 2 parts leaf mold or peat moss. A pH of 5.5 to 6.5 is ideal.

Indoors, provide very bright indirect or curtain-filtered sunlight such as that reflected from light walls (800 foot-candles). Temperatures of 50° to 60° at night, 70° to 80° by day, and 60 per cent humidity are best. Use a mixture of equal parts packaged potting soil, leaf mold or peat moss, and builder's sand; add 2 tablespoons of bone meal per gallon of mix. Do not fertilize newly purchased or repotted plants for six months; feed established ferns twice during the spring and early summer growing season using fish emulsion diluted to half the strength recommended on the label. Propagate the adder's-tongue fern by dividing the underground roots; 2- to 3-inch root segments will form buds and new plants when detached from the mother plant.

OPHIOGLOSSUM See also *Lygodium*
ORIENTAL WATER FERN See *Ceratopteris*

OSMUNDA

O. cinnamomea (cinnamon fern); *O. claytonia* (interrupted fern); *O. regalis* (royal fern)

Botanically, the osmunda ferns form a link between the modern and the ancient ferns that forested the earth in prehistoric times. They form large crowns of slightly erect stems with massive root systems, which are shredded and used as a growing medium for orchids and other air plants, including certain tropical ferns. Osmundas are among the earliest ferns to poke through the earth in spring, and their distinct crosiers, so matted with woolly hairs that they resemble cotton balls, are easy to identify.

Cinnamon ferns have separate sterile and fertile fronds. The fertile ones, which are the first to grow in the spring, have narrow leaflets that hug the stalks so closely that the frond looks like a club. These turn from green to brown as they mature in early spring, then wither and fall after they shed their spores. The sterile fronds, which unfurl slightly later in spring, remain green all summer until they are killed by frost. The erect fronds, growing in vase-shaped clusters 2 to 5 feet tall, have woolly tufts where the 4-inch pointed leaflets join the rib down the center of the frond.

The interrupted fern takes its common name from the odd location of its fertile leaflets. Several pairs of leaflets in the middle of each frond, greatly reduced in size and heavily covered with spore cases, shed their spores and wither in early summer. When they drop, they leave an empty space or interruption in the middle of the frond. The rest of the frond's 3- to 4-inch leaflets are sterile, and remain green until the fronds die back after frost.

The 6-foot royal fern is one of the largest native American species. Its elongated, blunt-tipped, 4-inch leaflets turn from red to green as they mature. Narrow fertile leaflets grow in brown clusters at the tip of each frond. The fern is deciduous except in parts of Zone 10 where some of its cultivated varieties remain green year round.

Distinctly different sterile and fertile parts make the slow-spreading osmunda ferns outstanding accent ferns in the garden border. Both the cinnamon fern and the royal fern grow luxuriantly in wet soils while the interrupted fern is better for drier sites. Their size and their need for winter cold, however, make them poor house plants.

HOW TO GROW. All of these ferns grow well in Zones 3-8 and the royal fern can be grown in Zone 9 and 10 as well. They grow best in deep shade but they will tolerate full sun if they receive plenty of moisture. Both the cinnamon and the royal ferns thrive in wet, boggy soils while the interrupted fern needs a slightly dry location. In preparing new garden beds for these ferns, use a mixture of 1 part garden loam, 1 part builder's sand and 2 parts leaf mold or peat moss; a pH of 5.5 to 6.5 is ideal.

Propagate these ferns by dividing their crowns in spring before new growth uncoils and plant the divisions 3 feet apart. All of these ferns can also be propagated by collecting their green spores in early summer and sowing them immediately on moist potting mix. These spores will grow only if they are fresh, but they germinate quickly, often in a day.

OSTRICH FERN See *Matteucia*

P

PARSLEY FERN See *Cryptogramma*

PELLAEA

P. atropurpurea (purple cliff brake); *P. brachyptera* (Sierra cliff brake); *P. densa,* also called *Aspidotis densa, Cheilanthes siliquosa, Onychium densum* (Indian's dream, cliff brake); *P. falcata* (Australian cliff brake); *P. rotundifolia* (button fern, New Zealand cliff brake); *P. viridis viridis,* also called *P. hastata* (green cliff brake)

In late spring, the crooklike crosiers of the cliff brake ferns push their way out from stone walls, or appear among rocks on dry ledges. These small- to medium-sized ferns with stiff, brittle purple or brown stems have different fertile and sterile fronds. The taller fertile fronds appear to have narrower leaves because the edges of the leaves curl back to protect the spore cases.

The 1½-foot purple cliff brake carries its narrow 3-inch leaflets at right angles to its purple stalks. With their stiff stalks and the wide spacing between their leaflets, the fronds look like miniature ladders. The evergreen, leathery leaflets change from green to gray-green to blue-green as they mature. This fern is an endangered species, which should not be collected in the wild.

The 16-inch Sierra cliff brake has leaflets that look like the needles on a fir tree. These leaflets stand out obliquely

For climate zones and frost dates, see maps, pages 146-147.

INTERRUPTED FERN
Osmunda claytonia

ROYAL FERN
Osmunda regalis

PURPLE CLIFF BRAKE
Pellaea atropurpurea

SIERRA CLIFF BRAKE
Pellaea brachyptera

INDIAN'S DREAM
Pellaea densa

BUTTON FERN
Pellaea rotundifolia

from powdery stalks that grow in clusters along a knotted stem. The tiny Indian's dream fern has 3-inch fronds only 1½ inches wide carried on 6-inch brown stalks. The triangular fertile fronds have narrow, oblong, pointed leaflets.

The Australian cliff brake has lance-shaped 1-foot fronds with broad, pointed 2-inch leaflets crowded along the stalks. As its name implies, the button fern has round, polished ½-inch leaflets attached to its wiry center rib on short stalks. The green cliff brake has broad triangular leaflets divided into three lobes. These 2-inch leaflets are carried on arching brown stalks up to 2 feet long.

Cliff brakes can be grown outdoors in a rock garden or as border plants. They are evergreen from Zone 6 south. Indoors they are highly ornamental in a small hanging basket, a pot or an open terrarium.

HOW TO GROW. Outdoors, the purple cliff brake, Sierra cliff brake and the Indian's dream fern grow best in Zones 3-8 in light shade. Plant the Australian cliff brake, button fern and the green cliff brake in Zones 7-10 in open shade. All six grow best when the soil is moist, even slightly dry. Wide fluctuations in moisture from bone dry to wet will weaken these ferns, and overwatering can kill them. To provide stable moisture conditions, it is sometimes necessary to grow them in separate outdoor beds, using a mixture of 1 part coarse sand to 1 part leaf mold or peat moss. A pH of 6.0 to 7.0 is best for all but the purple cliff brake. Add approximately 2 tablespoons of limestone to each cubic foot of soil used for the purple cliff brake to raise the pH to the 7.0 to 8.0 that suits it best.

Indoors, grow the purple cliff brake, Sierra cliff brake and Indian's dream fern in bright indirect or curtain-filtered sunlight (400 foot-candles) where night temperatures are 45° to 55° and day temperatures are 65° to 75°. The Australian cliff brake, button fern and green cliff brake do best in very bright indirect light such as that reflected from light walls (800 foot-candles) where night temperatures are 50° to 60° and day temperatures are 70° to 80°. Humidity of 40 per cent or less is best for all six. Use a mixture of equal parts builder's sand and leaf mold or peat moss. For a lighter mix in hanging baskets, use perlite or vermiculite in place of sand. Add 1 tablespoon of ground limestone to either mix when growing the purple cliff brake. Fertilize ferns once a month during the spring and summer growing season using fish emulsion diluted to half the strength recommended on the label. Propagate these ferns from spores or by dividing their rhizomes in spring before new growth appears.

PELLAEA See also *Doryopteris*
PEPPERWORT See *Marsilea*
PESSOPTERIS See *Polypodium*
PHLEBODIUM See *Polypodium*

PHYLLITIS

P. scolopendrium, also called *Scolopendrium vulgare, Asplenium scolopendrium* (hart's-tongue fern)

Perhaps the rarest of American ferns, the hart's-tongue is found in Tennessee, New York and near Owen Sound, Ontario. Only a few growers offer the American variety for sale. However, its British counterpart of the same species name is available in several fancy crested varieties and often sold in plant shops. The broad, 1- to 2-inch-wide fronds have heart-shaped bases, pointed tips, and are leathery in texture. They grow up to 1½ feet long. Circular tufts of 20 or more evergreen fronds hide the short, stout stems. The variety *crispifolium* has tight, curly waves along its edges; *crispum* has slightly wavy edges and tufts at the base of each frond;

GREEN CLIFF BRAKE
Pellaea viridis viridis

HART'S-TONGUE FERN
Phyllitis scolopendrium

For climate zones and frost dates, see maps, pages 146-147.

GOLDBACK FERN
Pityrogramma argentea

SILVER FERN
Pityrogramma calomelanos

cristatum is a compact cultivated variety with curly, ruffled leaf edges. The hart's-tongue fern is used outdoors in rock gardens or as a border planting. It also makes a good pot plant if the humidity can be kept high.

HOW TO GROW. Outdoors the hart's-tongue fern will grow in Zones 3-8 in deep shade. The soil should be constantly moist but not wet. In preparing a new bed, use a mixture of 1 part garden loam, 1 part builder's sand and 2 parts leaf mold or peat moss, adding 2 tablespoons of ground limestone per cubic foot of soil to achieve a pH of 7.0 to 8.0.

Indoors, the hart's-tongue fern will grow in low levels of indirect light such as that in a north window (150 foot-candles). It grows best when temperatures are 45° to 55° at night, 65° to 75° by day, and the humidity is 60 per cent or more. Keep the soil moist but not soggy and use a mixture of equal parts packaged potting soil, leaf mold or peat moss, and builder's sand; add 2 tablespoons of bone meal and 1 tablespoon of ground limestone per gallon of mix. Do not fertilize newly purchased or repotted plants for six months; feed established plants twice during the spring and summer growing season using fish emulsion fertilizer diluted to half the strength recommended on the label.

The hart's-tongue fern can be propagated by division or from spores, although plants grown from spores may look quite different from the parent plant. This fern can also be propagated by cutting the base of a leafstalk into pieces that are then placed on moist potting mix and grown under the same conditions as spores. Small bulbils appear along these pieces of stalk in two to three months. These may be planted in community containers until the plants are large enough to pot individually.

PINE FERN See *Anemia*

PITYROGRAMMA

P. argentea, also called *Ceratopteris argentea* (goldback fern); *P. calomelanos* (silver fern); *P. chrysophylla* (gold fern); *P. triangularis* (California goldback fern)

The colorful evergreen fronds of pityrogrammas secrete a powdery white, yellow, orange or red substance that gives each species its common name. Natives of rocky woods or dry shrubby slopes, these plants are good for rock gardens and can be used indoors in pots or hanging baskets.

The goldback fern's 1- to 3-foot fronds are carried on short 2- to 3-inch brown stalks. The backs of the fragile fronds are covered with white to red powder and the lowest leaflets are deltoid, resembling butterfly wings. The 3-foot-tall silver fern has white powder on the backs of its fronds that are about the same length as the stalks. The gold fern is similar to the silver fern except that it has smaller fronds with yellow powder on their undersides. The California goldback has 3- to 6-inch fronds with orange to white powder underneath that are carried on 6- to 18-inch stalks. Like the goldback fern, its lower leaflets are wing shaped.

HOW TO GROW. The goldback fern, silver fern and gold fern can be grown outdoors in Zone 10 while the California goldback fern will grow in Zones 8-10. All four ferns do best in open shade to full sun where the soil is moist to slightly dry. The California goldback fern will grow in drier soil than the other three. These ferns are sensitive to moisture fluctuations. Do not allow them to become bone dry and plant them in well-drained soils that will not become soggy after it has rained. To provide proper moisture conditions, it may be necessary to prepare a separate bed in the garden using 1 part builder's sand to 1 part leaf mold or peat moss. A pH of 5.5 to 6.5 is ideal.

Indoors, they do best in very bright indirect or curtain-filtered sunlight such as that reflected from light walls (800 foot-candles). They will also tolerate a few hours of direct sun each day. All but the California goldback fern do best when night temperatures are 60° to 70° and day temperatures are 75° to 80°; the California goldback fern does better in temperatures about 5° to 10° cooler than this. All thrive when humidity is 40 per cent or less. Keep the soil barely moist, a little on the dry side. Overwatering can kill these ferns. In pots, plant them in equal parts leaf mold or peat moss and builder's sand; for a lighter mix to use in hanging baskets, use perlite or vermiculite in place of the sand. Fertilize them monthly during the spring and summer growing season with fish emulsion diluted to half the strength recommended on the label. Remove old fronds as they wither. Propagate these ferns from spores or by division in spring before new growth begins.

PLATYCERIUM

P. angolense (Angola staghorn fern, elephant's-ear fern); *P. bifurcatum* (staghorn fern); *P. grande*, also called *P. superbum*; *P. hillii*; *P. vassei*, also called *P. alcicorne*; *P. willinckii* (Java staghorn fern)

The staghorn ferns are tropical air plants named for the shape of the gray or green fertile fronds, which may hang down 1 to 10 feet. Closely packed spore masses appear on the undersides of the "antlers" near the tips, covering them with soft brown fuzz when they are mature. The long fertile fronds grow from the center of smaller, overlapping sterile fronds, which clasp the tree or support on which the fern grows. These upright sterile fronds are green when they are young and turn brown as they age. In the wild they collect debris that provides the fern with nutrients and help to hold moisture. New plants called pups form amid the sterile fronds of some plants.

The Angola staghorn from Africa is one of the largest species, bearing huge wedge-shaped fertile fronds, which, unlike the other species, are undivided and resemble elephant ears. Dark veins line their upper surfaces and the velvety undersides are covered with hairs.

The common staghorn fern, *P. bifurcatum*, has dangling leathery fertile fronds up to 3 feet long with finger-like divisions at their ends; San Diego staghorn is a popular cultivar with fingers that are broader and more rounded than those of *P. bifurcatum*. *P. grande* has fan-shaped sterile leaves 4 to 5 feet wide standing above 3-foot fertile fronds. *P. hillii*'s kidney-shaped sterile fronds hug the fern's rootstock while the erect fertile fronds fan out into dark green fingers. *P. vassei* is a compact species from Mozambique whose short, stiff, 12-inch fertile fronds grow upright instead of hanging. Both the sterile and fertile fronds of the Java staghorn are deeply forked; the trailing 4-foot fertile fronds have white hairs that make the fronds look silvered.

Attach these unusual ferns to trees outdoors or hang them on slabs of bark or in baskets. Although their drooping fertile fronds are shown to best advantage when the ferns are hung on slabs or in baskets, they can be grown as pot plants. Indoors, take care to position hanging ferns where water dripping from the base will not damage furnishings.

HOW TO GROW. Grow the Angola staghorn fern, *P. vassei* and the Java staghorn outdoors in Zone 10. *P. bifurcatum* and its cultivars such as the San Diego staghorn fern, *P. grande* and *P. hillii* will grow in Zones 7-10. Give them all open shade and keep them moist, a little on the dry side.

Indoors, provide bright to very bright indirect or curtain-filtered sunlight (400 to 800 foot-candles). Temperatures of

For climate zones and frost dates, see maps, pages 146-147.

CALIFORNIA GOLDBACK FERN
Pityrogramma triangularis

ANGOLA STAGHORN FERN
Platycerium angolense

SAN DIEGO STAGHORN FERN
Platycerium bifurcatum 'San Diego'

Platycerium vassei

60° to 70° at night and 75° to 80° by day are ideal, although *P. bifurcatum*, its cultivars, *P. grande* and *P. hillii* will thrive at temperatures 10° cooler than this. Humidity of 50 to 60 per cent is ideal for all of them.

These ferns can be grown on a variety of organic materials that retain moisture. Attach them to a living tree, a bark-covered slab of wood, a piece of cork bark or a section of tree fern trunk. Place the plant on long-fibered sphagnum moss, or a combination of tree fern fiber or osmunda fern fiber with sphagnum moss, and anchor it to the base with nylon fish line or plastic-coated wire. When anchoring a fern to a living tree, use strips of nylon stockings or any other pliant cord to avoid damaging the tree's bark. In hanging baskets or pots, use a mixture of coarse peat moss and long-fibered sphagnum moss. A pH of 6.0 to 7.0 is ideal. Water the fern by soaking it in a sink or pail of water once or twice a week during hot weather, every week or two when it is cooler, and spray the foliage when watering. Avoid overwatering. Fertilize twice a year during the spring and summer growing season by adding fish emulsion to the water the fern is soaked in at half the rate recommended on the label.

Propagate these ferns at any time by spores or by removing and rooting small plants that develop under the basal fronds of all but *P. grande*.

PLEURIDIUM See *Polypodium*
POLYNESIAN DAVALLIA See *Davallia*

POLYPODIUM

P. angustifolium, also called *Campyloneurum angustifolium* (narrow-leaved strap fern); *P. aureum,* also called *Phlebodium aureum* (rabbit's-foot fern, golden polypody); *P. coronans,* also called *Aglaomorpha coronans, Polypodium conjugatum, Drynaria conjugata; P. crassifolium,* also called *Pessopteris crassifolium, Pleuridium crassifolium; P. glycyrrhiza,* also called *P. vulgare occidentale* (licorice fern); *P. lycopodioides; P. polycarpon grandiceps* (climbing bird's-nest fern); *P. polypodioides* (resurrection fern, little gray polypody); *P. scouleri,* also called *Goniophlebium scouleri* (leathery polypody, leatherleaf); *P. subauriculatum,* also called *Schellolepis subauriculata* (jointed polypody); *P. vulgare* (common polypody, adder's fern, brakeroot, wall fern) (all called polypody)

Polypodium is a large genus of more than 1,000 species, most of them slow growing and moderately easy to cultivate. Their leathery fronds spring from creeping stems and leave a scar when they wither and drop off. Their spores form round clusters in single or double rows along the underside of each leaflet. Because of the polypodies' shallow root systems they can be grown in low pots or pans. They are good hanging-basket plants and are sometimes used outdoors in rock gardens or as accent plants.

The narrow-leaved strap fern forms clumps of thin, ribbon-like 12- to 18-inch fronds with rolled edges. The rabbit's-foot fern has deeply cut fronds, 2 or more feet long, growing along a thick, fuzzy and scaly stem that resembles a rabbit's foot as it creeps over the edge of a pot; golden polypody derives its name from the gold color of this fern's spores. This polypody has a number of cultivars including *P. aureum mandaianum,* Manda's golden polypody, or the blue fern, with pendulous blue-green curly-edged fronds; the Mexican tasseled golden polypody with frond tips forked into heavy crests; and *undulatum,* a compact cultivar with fronds divided into broad, wavy-edged blue-green leaflets. *P. coronans,* a coarse, expansive fern, has stiff, glossy 1- to 1½-foot fronds that form clumps 4 to 6 feet across; the base of each

For climate zones and frost dates, see maps, pages 146-147.

NARROW-LEAVED STRAP FERN
Polypodium angustifolium

RABBIT'S-FOOT FERN
Polypodium aureum

Polypodium coronans

Polypodium crassifolium

LICORICE FERN
Polypodium glycyrrhiza

Polypodium lycopodioides

CLIMBING BIRD'S-NEST FERN
Polypodium polycarpon grandiceps

LEATHERY POLYPODY
Polypodium scouleri

frond is wide and papery, browning as the frond matures. *P. crassifolium* bears strap-shaped fronds 1 to 3 feet long and 1 to 5 inches wide; the surface of these short-stalked, wavy-edged leaves is spotted with white.

The licorice fern occasionally appears mixed into moss shipped from the western states where it grows wild; named for the taste of its spreading stems, it has 1- to 3-foot deciduous fronds with pointed leaflets. The dwarf and trailing *P. lycopodioides* has one-piece oval and pointed fronds that are only 2 to 4 inches long and ½ to 1 inch wide. The climbing bird's-nest fern has unusual thick fronds 1 to 2 feet long and 1 to 2 inches wide that in one cultivated variety fan out into pointed, irregularly forked tips up to 6 inches across. The resurrection fern's 7-inch fronds become dry and curl into balls during periods of drought, then uncoil and turn green when the moisture returns; gray scales cover the undersides of the leathery leaflets. Leathery polypody's waxy 1- to 3-foot fronds are deeply cut into round-tipped leaflets. Jointed polypody has shiny, pendulous fronds 4 to 8 feet long that are used as foliage in cut flower arrangements. Common polypody forms thick mats of fronds 6 to 12 inches long and 2 inches wide with thin, wavy-edged leaflets; during the winter, the leaflets curl up to expose their backs and the mature spores on them.

In Europe, the name wall fern is given to *P. vulgare*, while in the United States, the name is applied to *P. virginianum*. The two ferns are essentially the same, except that the spore cases of the European wall fern occur at the leaflet edges while those of the American wall fern are about halfway between the edge of the leaflet and the rib down its center.

HOW TO GROW. Licorice fern and common polypody grow outdoors in Zones 3-8; the leathery polypody in Zones 5-10. The narrow-leaved strap fern, the rabbit's-foot fern, *P. coronans* and the resurrection fern grow outdoors in Zones 9 and 10; *P. crassifolium, P. lycopodioides,* the climbing bird's-nest fern and the jointed polypody in Zone 10. The rabbit's-foot fern and *P. coronans* grow best in open shade while all of the others do best in light shade. All should be planted in well-drained soils that are constantly moist but not wet. In preparing new beds, use a mixture of 1 part garden loam, 1 part builder's sand and 2 parts leaf mold or peat moss. A pH of 5.5 to 6.5 is ideal.

Indoors, provide very bright indirect or curtain-filtered sunlight such as that reflected from light walls (800 foot-candles) for the rabbit's-foot fern and *P. coronans,* less light for the others (400 foot-candles). Night temperatures of 50° to 60° and day temperatures of 70° to 80° suit most of them. The licorice fern and the common polypody will thrive at temperatures 5° to 10° cooler. All do best when humidity is 50 to 60 per cent. Keep them moist but not soggy in a mixture of 1 part peat moss or leaf mold, 1 part builder's sand and 2 parts perlite or vermiculite; add 2 tablespoons of bone meal per gallon of this mix. Do not fertilize newly purchased or repotted plants for six months; feed established plants twice during the spring and summer growing season, using fish emulsion diluted to half the strength recommended on the label. For a lighter mix in hanging baskets, omit the sand and use equal parts peat moss or leaf mold and perlite or vermiculite. Feed baskets monthly during the growing season with fish emulsion used half strength.

Propagate polypodies by dividing the creeping stems and pinning them to the surface of moist potting mix until new roots have formed. They can also be grown from spores. The rabbit's-foot fern grows very rapidly from spores and its off-spring frequently have new characteristics, such as ruffled edges, distinct from those of the parent plant.

For climate zones and frost dates, see maps, pages 146-147.

JOINTED POLYPODY
Polypodium subauriculatum

COMMON POLYPODY
Polypodium vulgare

CHRISTMAS FERN
Polystichum acrostichoides

LEATHER FERN
Polystichum adiantiforme

POLYPODIUM See also *Drynaria*
POLYPODY See *Polypodium*

POLYSTICHUM

P. acrostichoides (Christmas fern); *P. adiantiforme*, also called *P. coriaceum, P. capense, Aspidium capense, Rumohra adiantiformis* (leather fern); *P. aristatum*, also called *Arachniodes aristata, Lastrea aristata* (East Indian holly fern); *P. munitum* (western sword fern); *P. setiferum*, also called *P. angulare* (soft shield fern); *P. standishii*, also called *Arachniodes standishii* (upside-down fern); *P. tsus-simense*, also called *Aspidium tsus-simense* (Tsussima holly fern)

Polystichums are robust ferns that form handsome, symmetrical crowns of fronds. Their leathery, evergreen foliage is frequently cut for use in floral arrangements and wreaths. These stiff, bushy ferns are used as border and foundation plants outdoors. As pot or basket plants indoors they will tolerate drafts except when they are actually growing during spring and summer.

The one-piece, 3-inch leaflets of the Christmas fern have a pointed or rounded bump called an ear on their topmost edge, close to the stalk; early settlers in the northeastern United States prized this fern's 1- to 3-foot fronds as holiday decorations and gave it its common name. The leather fern has coarsely lobed 12- to 20-inch fronds that become very rough and stiff with age. The East Indian holly fern has oval 1½- to 3-foot fronds up to 1 foot wide; the tapering, harsh-textured leaflets end in spiny segments and the lower leaflets are shaped like butterflies. The western sword fern has pairs of 5-inch dagger-shaped leaflets that have bristly, prickly edges; these ferns grow 1½ to 3 feet tall and older clumps may have as many as 75 to 100 fronds. The soft shield fern has more pliant and arching stalks than those of other polystichum species; the foliage is finely divided on lacy fronds that are 1 to 2½ feet long.

Most ferns have prominent veins on the undersurface of their fronds; the veins of the upside-down fern, however, protrude from the top surface, giving the fern its common name. The 1- to 3-foot fronds are cut into three segments with extremely lacy leaflets. The Tsussima holly fern has 6- to 12-inch tapering fronds whose leathery leaflets are tipped with needle-sharp spines. This dwarf polystichum species is popular for dish gardens and terrariums.

HOW TO GROW. The Christmas fern can be grown outdoors in Zones 3-8; grow the others in Zones 7-10. The leather fern, East Indian holly fern, soft shield fern, the upside-down fern and the Tsussima holly fern grow best in light shade while the Christmas fern and western sword fern will grow in deep shade. All do best when the soil is constantly moist but not soggy. In preparing a new bed, use a mixture of 1 part garden loam, 1 part builder's sand and 2 parts leaf mold or peat moss. A pH of 5.5 to 6.6 is best.

Indoors, provide bright indirect or curtain-filtered sunlight (400 foot-candles). The Christmas and western sword ferns will tolerate very low indirect light (150 foot-candles). Temperatures of 45° to 55° at night and 65° to 75° by day are ideal for all except the leather fern, which prefers temperatures about 5° warmer than these. Humidity of 60 per cent or more is best for all of them. Keep them moist but not wet in a mixture of equal parts packaged potting soil, leaf mold or peat moss, and builder's sand; add 2 tablespoons of bone meal to each gallon of this mix. Do not fertilize newly purchased or repotted plants for six months; feed established plants twice during the spring and summer growing season with fish-emulsion fertilizer diluted to half the strength recommended on the label.

For climate zones and frost dates, see maps, pages 146-147.

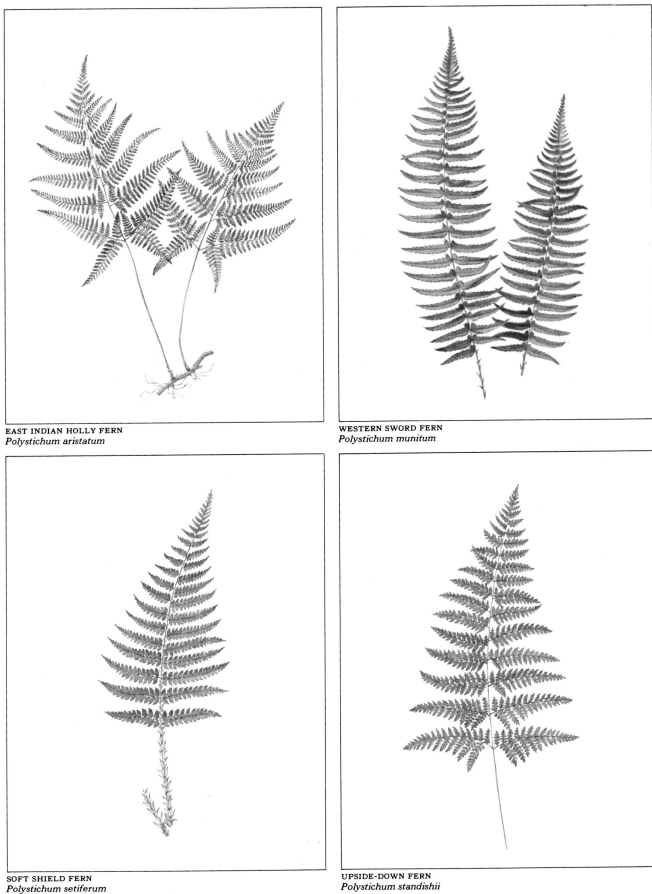

EAST INDIAN HOLLY FERN
Polystichum aristatum

WESTERN SWORD FERN
Polystichum munitum

SOFT SHIELD FERN
Polystichum setiferum

UPSIDE-DOWN FERN
Polystichum standishii

EASTERN BRACKEN FERN
Pteridium aquilinum latiusculum

SILVER BRAKE FERN
Pteris biaurita argyraea

Propagate these ferns by dividing their crowns in spring or growing them from spores. Spores will grow into plants that are ready for 2½-inch pots within a year.

PTERETIS See *Matteuccia*

PTERIDIUM
P. aquilinum (bracken fern, brake fern)

The genus *Pteridium* contains only one worldwide species, *P. aquilinum,* but it is highly variable and different varieties occur in different parts of the world. The three most common varieties found in the United States are *pubescens* or western bracken with hairy stalks and a tuft of dark hairs at the growing tip of its underground stem; *latiusculum* or eastern bracken with a white-haired growing tip; and *pseudocaudatum* with hairless stalks and dark hairs at the growing tip. All three varieties are found throughout the United States, but as their common names imply, eastern and western bracken are more usual in those regions of the country while *pseudocaudatum* is most common in the East, the Southeast and throughout the Gulf Coast states.

Bracken ferns grow in open woods, fields or thickets and their presence usually signals poor soil. When the crosiers first uncurl in the spring, they resemble eagle claws covered with white-gray hairs. They develop into coarse, leathery, triangular fronds, 1 to 2 feet long and equally wide, growing on woody stalks 1 to 3 feet tall. Leaflet edges roll back and under to protect the fern's spore cases. The fronds grow at irregular intervals along a hairy, creeping stem that has deep roots which soon invade other nearby areas. Although some gardeners regard them as weeds because of this spreading habit, bracken ferns are easily grown knee-high ground covers for barren areas. They are not grown as pot plants because of their size and coarseness.

HOW TO GROW. Although bracken ferns will grow in acidic soils in Zones 3-10 under almost any conditions of light and moisture, they grow best in open shade in moist to slightly dry soils. For a new bed, use a mixture of 1 part garden loam, 1 part builder's sand and 2 parts leaf mold or peat moss. A pH of 5.5 to 6.5 is ideal. These ferns can be grown from spores, but they are most easily propagated by dividing their underground stems and setting divisions 3 feet apart.

PTERIS
P. biaurita, also called *P. quadriaurita; P. cretica* (Cretan brake fern); *P. ensiformis,* also called *P. chinensis* (sword brake fern); *P. multifida,* also called *P. serrulata* (spider brake fern); *P. tremula* (trembling or Australian brake fern) (all called table fern, brake fern, stove fern)

In other countries, table ferns enjoy the same degree of renown as house plants that Americans accord the Boston fern. Like *Nephrolepis exaltata bostoniensis* and its cultivars, table ferns are adaptable, easy to grow, and have species bred into numerous varieties with frilled, crested, crimped and otherwise fancied-up leaflets. The shape of their fronds also adds interest to the plants. The lowest pair of leaflets on each frond is divided so that it resembles butterfly wings. While these ferns are excellent house plants, they can also be used in a dish garden or terrarium. Larger species are valued by florists and interior decorators for use as sculpturesque floor plants. These same shapely silhouettes make table ferns striking accent plants in the garden. Tuck smaller plants into rock gardens or use them as bedding plants. *P. biaurita* is a robust 2- to 3-foot fern with leathery leaflets. *P. biaurita argyraea,* the silver brake fern, has streaks of white down the center of each deeply lobed leaflet.

There are numerous frilled and crested variations of the Cretan brake fern's 6- to 12-inch papery fronds. *P. cretica albo-lineata*, the ribbon brake, has a cream or white streak running down the center of its broad tapering leaflets; *P. cretica* Distinction has leaflets that fork so many times that the fronds become lacy and bushy; *P. cretica wilsonii* has fan-shaped fronds with heavily crested tips. The sword brake fern has two kinds of fronds; the spreading 9- to 18-inch sterile fronds have elliptical leaflets while the erect fertile ones have wavy edges. *P. ensiformis victoriae*, the Victorian brake, is a dwarf cultivar with silvery-white bands down the center of each leaflet. Spider brake is a 1- to 2-foot plant with willowy fronds divided many times into very narrow, long leaflets. Table fern is a misnomer for the trembling brake fern. Although young plants make attractive table displays, mature ones reach 3 to 4 feet and are more suitable as floor plants. The coarse, deeply lobed leaflets overlap one another and new crosiers unfold with such regularity that a few older fronds are always available for cut foliage.

HOW TO GROW. Grow brake ferns outdoors in Zones 7-10 in light shade where the soil stays constantly moist but not soggy. In preparing new beds, use a mixture of 1 part garden loam, 1 part builder's sand, and 2 parts leaf mold or peat moss. A pH of 5.5 to 6.5 is ideal.

Indoors, these ferns do best in bright indirect or curtain-filtered sunlight (400 foot-candles). Night temperatures of 50° to 60°, day temperatures of 70° to 80°, and 60 per cent humidity are ideal. Pot in a mixture of equal parts packaged potting soil, builder's sand and peat moss or leaf mold; add 2 tablespoons of bone meal to each gallon of soil mix. Keep the soil constantly moist. Do not feed newly potted or newly purchased plants for six months; fertilize established plants twice a year during the spring and summer growing season with fish emulsion diluted to half the strength recommended on the label. Cut off older, tattered leaves.

Propagate at any time by dividing the base of the plant. These plants are easily grown from spores and new plantlets frequently start from spores that fall on a moist soil surface or the sides of clay pots in greenhouses.

PTERIS See also *Doryopteris*
PURPLE CLIFF BRAKE See *Pellaea*
PYRROSIA See *Cyclophorus*

R

RABBIT'S-FOOT FERN See *Polypodium*
RATTLESNAKE FERN See *Botrychium*
RESURRECTION FERN See *Polypodium*
ROCK BRAKE, AMERICAN See *Cryptogramma*
ROSY or ROUGH MAIDENHAIR See *Adiantum*
ROYAL FERN See *Osmunda*
RUMOHRA See *Polystichum*
RUSH See *Equisetum*
RUSTY-BACK FERN See *Ceterach*
RUSTY CLIFF FERN See *Woodsia*
RUSTY WOODSIA See *Woodsia*

S

SAGENIA See *Tectaria*
SAGO TREE FERN See *Cyathea*

SALVINIA
S. natans, also called *S. auriculata*; *S. rotundifolia* (water spangles)

These attractive floating plants have tiny ½-inch leaves paired along their stems. The oval leaves of *S. natans* crowd

For climate zones and frost dates, see maps, pages 146-147.

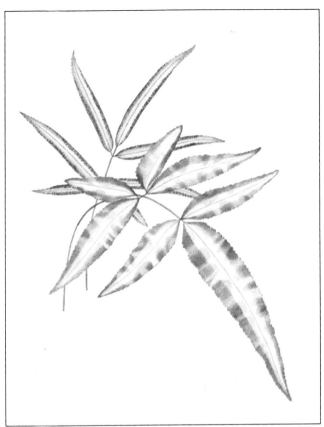

RIBBON BRAKE FERN
Pteris cretica albo-lineata

SPIDER BRAKE FERN
Pteris multifida

Salvinia natans

MONKEY'S-PAW FERN
Scyphularia pentaphylla

along their stems on short stalks while the round leaves of water spangles are carried away from the stems on long stalks. The upper surfaces of the leaves are covered with stiff hairs that help to keep them from becoming waterlogged. The threadlike fibers dangling in the water are not roots but greatly modified and divided leaves. The plants bear both male and female spores in clusters that hang underwater. These tropical ferns spread rapidly, forming sizable new colonies in just a season. Use them in an outdoor pool, or grow them indoors in an aquarium or terrarium.

HOW TO GROW. Grow these ferns outdoors in light shade in Zones 7-10 in still or slow-moving, shallow water. Water containing some organic matter and a pH of 7.0 is best.

Indoors provide bright indirect or curtain-filtered sunlight (400 foot-candles), air temperatures ranging from 50° to 80° and water temperatures of 70° to 75°. In shallow dishes in a terrarium, use equal parts packaged potting soil, builder's sand and peat moss or leaf mold; cover with ½ inch of water or float them in an aquarium containing some organic matter at the bottom. Propagate at any time by dividing plants.

SCALE FERN See *Ceterach*
SCHELLOLEPIS See *Polypodium*
SCOLOPENDRIUM See *Phyllitis*
SCOURING RUSH See *Equisetum*

SCYPHULARIA

S. pentaphylla, also called *Davallia pentaphylla* (monkey's-paw fern)

The 9- to 12-inch fronds of the monkey's-paw fern are composed of paired tapering leaflets. Sterile leaves have saw-toothed edges while fertile ones are wavy-edged. During the late summer or early fall the fronds turn a decorative yellow color and then wither, but they are soon replaced by green new growth. The wiry, hairy stems running along the surface of the ground can be trained to climb stakes or left to dangle from hanging baskets.

HOW TO GROW. Grow the monkey's-paw fern outdoors in Zone 10 in moist to slightly dry soil in open shade. In preparing a new bed, use 1 part garden loam, 1 part builder's sand and 2 parts leaf mold or peat moss. A pH of 6.0 to 7.0 is ideal for this fern.

Indoors, the monkey's-paw fern does best in very bright indirect or curtain-filtered sunlight such as that reflected from light walls (800 foot-candles). Night temperatures of 60° to 70°, day temperatures of 75° to 80°, and 50 to 60 per cent humidity are ideal. In pots, use a mixture of 1 part leaf mold or peat moss, 1 part builder's sand and 2 parts perlite or vermiculite; add 2 tablespoons of bone meal per gallon of mix. Do not feed newly potted or newly purchased plants for six months; feed established plants twice a year during the spring and summer growing season with fish emulsion diluted to half the strength recommended on the label. For a lighter mix in hanging baskets, omit the sand and use equal parts of leaf mold or peat moss and perlite or vermiculite; feed baskets monthly during the growing season with fish emulsion used half strength. Keep the growing medium barely moist at all times. Cut off yellow fronds when they begin to wither to stimulate new growth. Repot ferns to larger containers in the spring only as necessary; with careful watering, monkey's-paw can remain potbound for several years. Propagate at any season by dividing the rhizomes and pinning them to moist potting soil with bent wire until they form roots, or start new plants from spores.

SCYTHIAN LAMB See *Cibotium*

SELAGINELLA

S. kraussiana, also called *S. denticulata* (spreading selaginella, spreading spikemoss)

Spreading selaginella forms mossy blankets of tiny scale-like ⅛-inch leaves on creeping stems. It is an easy-to-grow ground cover in rock gardens and will quickly carpet a terrarium or overflow a pot when grown indoors. The creeping stems sprout tiny roots as they travel and bear separate male and female spores in cone-shaped clusters at their tips. Some varieties have yellow-green leaves *(S. kraussiana aurea)* or white-tipped leaves *(S. kraussiana variegata).* A dwarf type *(S. kraussiana brownii)* forms small cushions of bright green foliage and will take over the space in a terrarium more slowly than the other fern cultivars.

HOW TO GROW. Grow spreading selaginella outdoors in Zones 7-10 in light shade where the soil is moist to wet. In preparing new beds use a mixture of 1 part garden loam to 1 part builder's sand to 2 parts leaf mold or peat moss. A pH of 5.5 to 6.6 is best.

Indoors, grow spreading selaginella in bright indirect or curtain-filtered sunlight (400 foot-candles). Temperatures of 50° to 60° at night, 70° to 80° by day, and relative humidity of 60 to 80 per cent are ideal. Pot in a mixture of equal parts packaged potting soil, leaf mold or peat moss, and builder's sand. Keep the soil evenly moist at all times. Fertilize twice a year during the spring and summer growing season using fish emulsion diluted to half the strength recommended on the label. Propagate at any time by pinning 1½-inch stem cuttings to moist sand and misting daily until new roots form.

SENSITIVE FERN See *Onoclea*
SHAMROCK, WATER See *Marsilea*
SHIELD FERN See *Dryopteris*
SIERRA CLIFF BRAKE See *Pellaea*
SILVER-DOLLAR FERN See *Adiantum*
SILVER FERN See *Pityrogramma*
SILVER TREE FERN See *Cyathea*
SILVERY GLADE FERN See *Athyrium*
SLENDER TREE FERN See *Dicksonia*
SOFT SHIELD FERN See *Polystichum*
SOUTHERN MAIDENHAIR See *Adiantum*
SPEAR-LEAVED FERN See *Doryopteris*
SPHAEROPTERIS See *Alsophila* and *Cyathea*
SPIDER BRAKE See *Pteris*
SPIKEMOSS, SPREADING See *Selaginella*
SPLEENWORT See *Asplenium*
SPREADING SELAGINELLA See *Selaginella*
SPREADING SPIKEMOSS See *Selaginella*
STAGHORN FERN See *Platycerium*
STAGHORN FERN, FLOATING See *Ceratopteris*
STOVE FERN See *Pteris*
STRAP FERN, NARROW-LEAVED See *Polypodium*
STRAWBERRY FERN See *Hemionitis*
SWAMP FERN See *Acrostichum*
SWORD BRAKE FERN See *Pteris*
SWORD FERN See *Nephrolepis*
SWORD FERN, WESTERN See *Polystichum*

T

TABLE FERN See *Pteris*
TASMANIAN DICKSONIA See *Dicksonia*
TASMANIAN TREE FERN See *Dicksonia*

TECTARIA

T. gemmifera, also called *T. cicutaria, Sagenia cicutaria* (button fern)

For climate zones and frost dates, see maps, pages 146-147.

SPREADING SELAGINELLA
Selaginella kraussiana

BUTTON FERN
Tectaria gemmifera

CRAPE FERN
Todea barbara

This button fern gets its name from the shape of the small buds that develop along the tips of its fronds and eventually produce new plantlets (the name button fern is also applied to *Pellaea rotundifolida* because of that fern's round leaflets). The scaly brown stalks rise 15 inches from a thickened underground stem and bear coarse triangular fronds up to 2½ feet long. The downy evergreen fertile and sterile fronds are identical except for the round or kidney-shaped spore cases on the backs of fertile ones. The button fern is used as a pot plant or as an accent or background plant in the garden. Some gardeners consider them a weed because their plantlets or bulbils drop off and take root wherever they fall.

HOW TO GROW. The button fern will grow outdoors in Zones 7-10 in light shade. The soil should be constantly moist, but not wet. In preparing a new bed, use a mixture of 1 part garden loam, 1 part builder's sand and 2 parts leaf mold or peat moss. A pH of 5.5 to 6.5 is best.

Indoors, provide bright indirect or curtain-filtered sunlight (400 foot-candles). Night temperature of 50° to 60°, day temperatures of 70° to 80°, and 60 per cent humidity are ideal. For best results indoors use a mixture of equal parts packaged potting soil, builder's sand and peat moss or leaf mold; add 2 tablespoons of bone meal per gallon of mix. Keep the soil moist. Do not feed newly potted or newly purchased plants for six months; feed established plants two times a year during the spring and summer growing season with fish emulsion fertilizer diluted to half the strength recommended on the label. Propagate at any season from the plantlets that develop on the fronds or from spores.

THELYPTERIS See *Dryopteris*

TODEA
T. barbara, also called *T. africana, T. arborea* (crape fern)

The crape fern forms a handsome wheel of arching, leathery fronds that makes it an unusually attractive pot plant. This evergreen fern also makes an excellent accent plant in the garden because its triangular, 1- to 3-foot fronds grow on erect stems that form clumps rather than spreading widely.

HOW TO GROW. The crape fern can be grown outdoors in Zones 7-10 in open shade. Plant in constantly moist but not wet beds made of 1 part garden loam, 1 part builder's sand and 2 parts leaf mold or peat moss with a pH of 5.5 to 6.5. Remove any dead leaves in the spring so they will not entangle new fronds.

Indoors, plants do best in very bright indirect or curtain-filtered sunlight such as that reflected from light walls (800 foot-candles). Night temperatures of 50° to 60°, day temperatures of 70° to 80°, and humidity of 60 per cent or more are ideal. Pot in a mixture of equal parts packaged potting soil, builder's sand and peat moss or leaf mold; add 2 tablespoons of bone meal per gallon of mix. Keep the soil moist at all times but not soggy. Do not feed newly purchased or repotted plants for six months; feed established plants twice during the spring and summer growing season with fish emulsion diluted to half the strength recommended on the label. Propagate at any season from spores or by dividing plants.

TONGUE FERN See *Cyclophorus*
TREE FERN, AMERICAN See *Dryopteris*
TREE FERN, AUSTRALIAN See *Alsophila*
TREE FERN, BLACK See *Cyathea*
TREE FERN, COOPER See *Alsophila*
TREE FERN, FLORIDA See *Dryopteris*
TREE FERN, HAWAIIAN See *Cibotium*
TREE FERN, MEXICAN See *Cibotium*

TREE FERN, SAGO See *Cyathea*
TREE FERN, SILVER See *Cyathea*
TREE FERN, SLENDER See *Dicksonia*
TREE FERN, TASMANIAN See *Dicksonia*
TREE FERN, WEST INDIAN See *Cyathea*
TREE FERN, WOOLLY See *Dicksonia*
TREMBLING BRAKE FERN See *Pteris*

TRICHOMANES

T. petersii; T. radicans, also called *T. boschianum* (bristle fern, filmy fern, Killarney fern, cup goldilocks)

T. petersii and the bristle fern are indeed filmy ferns, their fronds so thin they are almost transparent. The bristle fern has fan-shaped leaflets on fronds 6 to 8 inches tall in contrast to the ½-inch height of *T. petersii.* The fronds of both ferns grow singly along threadlike underground stems. These ferns carry their spores in tube-shaped depressions along the edges of their leaflets. They grow slowly and are difficult to cultivate. As a result, they are not widely sold, and fern growers usually obtain these ferns by swapping with other enthusiasts for divisions to propagate new plants.

HOW TO GROW. These ferns do best in a covered terrarium in a very low level of indirect or curtain-filtered sunlight such as that in a north window (150 foot-candles). Night temperatures of 50° to 60° and day temperatures of 70° to 80° are ideal. They need 100 per cent humidity and soil that is always moist but not soggy; mist them weekly. The combination of high humidity and warm temperatures can stimulate fungus growth unless the terrarium is ventilated by removing the cover for a few minutes every few weeks. Plant the fern on tree fern fiber or anchor the threadlike stems to rocks with nylon fish line and moss. Fertilize once a year while the fern is actively growing, using fish emulsion at half the strength recommended on the label.

Propagate by dividing the stem just before new growth resumes in early spring. Anchor plants in position with nylon fish line or plastic-coated wire until new roots grow.

TSUSSIMA HOLLY FERN See *Polystichum*

U

UPSIDE-DOWN FERN See *Polystichum*

V

VARIEGATED SCOURING RUSH See *Equisetum*
VEGETABLE FERN See *Diplazium*
VENUS'S MAIDENHAIR See *Adiantum*
VIRGINIA CHAIN FERN See *Woodwardia*

W

WALKING FERN See *Camptosorus*
WALL FERN See *Polypodium*
WATER CLOVER FERN See *Marsilea*
WATER FERN, AMERICAN See *Ceratopteris*
WATER FERN, ORIENTAL See *Ceratopteris*
WATER SHAMROCK See *Marsilea*
WATER SPANGLES See *Salvinia*
WATER SPRITE See *Ceratopteris*
WEST INDIAN TREE FERN See *Cyathea*
WESTERN SWORD FERN See *Polystichum*
WOOD FERN, COASTAL See *Dryopteris*

WOODSIA

W. ilvensis (rusty woodsia, rusty cliff fern); *W. obtusa,* also called *W. perriniana* (blunt-lobed woodsia, blunt-lobed cliff fern); *W. scopulina* (mountain woodsia)

For climate zones and frost dates, see maps, pages 146-147.

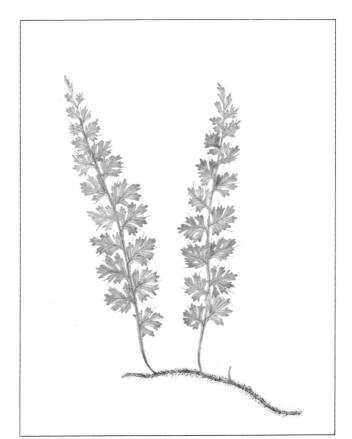

BRISTLE FERN
Trichomanes radicans

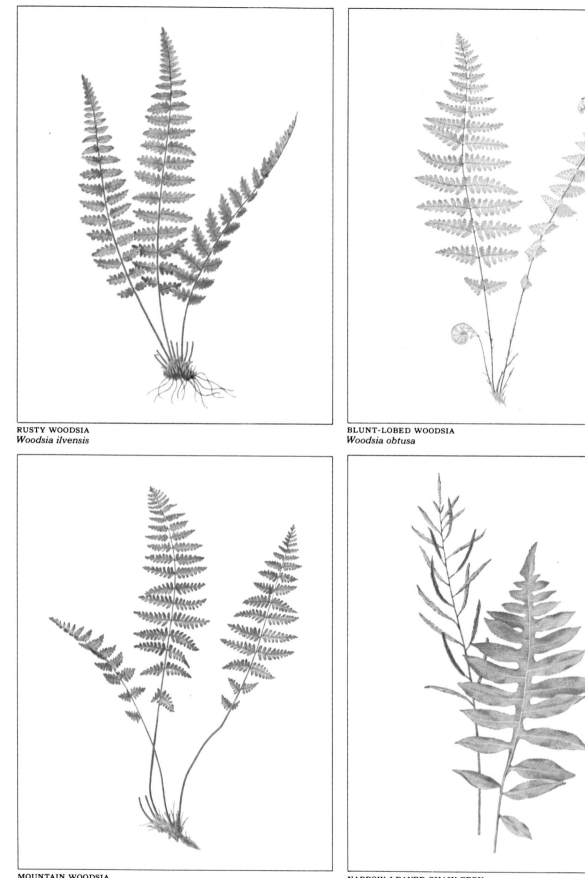

RUSTY WOODSIA
Woodsia ilvensis

BLUNT-LOBED WOODSIA
Woodsia obtusa

MOUNTAIN WOODSIA
Woodsia scopulina

NARROW-LEAVED CHAIN FERN
Woodwardia areolata

Delicate woodsias are excellent rock garden ferns that will grow in even the poorest soil. Their fertile and sterile fronds rise in erect clusters from short, scaly thickened stems and are almost identical except for the spore cases on the undersides of fertile fronds. When the spores mature in the late spring and early summer, these cases split open to resemble many-pointed stars and flowers.

Tiny rusty woodsia has lacy 3- to 6-inch fronds only 1 inch wide that are smooth on top and covered with brown hairs and scales underneath. The shaggy brown stalks are jointed. Blunt-lobed woodsia has round-tipped leaflets with white hairs above and below that sometimes make the fronds appear gray. Blunt-lobed woodsia and mountain woodsia both have unjointed stalks and stand 6 to 8 inches tall. Mountain woodsia, which has toothed leaflets that are cut more deeply than those of blunt-lobed woodsia, has a more raggedy appearance. These three woodsia ferns are deciduous north of Zone 6, evergreen south of it. They do not do well as indoor pot plants.

HOW TO GROW. Grow woodsias outdoors in Zones 3-8 in light shade. They do best among rocks in soils that are moist to slightly wet. Blunt-lobed woodsia does well along masonry walls where it benefits from the limestone in the mortar. In preparing a new bed, use a mixture of 1 part garden loam, 1 part builder's sand and 2 parts leaf mold or peat moss. A pH of 5.5 to 6.5 is best for the rusty and mountain woodsia, but add approximately 2 tablespoons of ground limestone to each cubic foot of soil used for the blunt-lobed woodsia to raise the pH to the 7.0 to 8.0 it needs. Propagate by dividing the underground stems in early spring or from spores.

WOODWARDIA

W. areolata, also called *Lorinseria areolata, W. angustifolia* (narrow-leaved chain fern, net-veined chain fern); *W. fimbriata,* also called *W. chamissoi, W. radicans americana* (giant chain fern); *W. virginica* (Virginia chain fern, Eastern chain fern)

Chain ferns are fast-spreading species especially suitable for difficult swampy locations. The double lines of spores on the backs of the fertile fronds inspired the common name chain fern. The deciduous fronds are spaced several inches apart on strong, forked underground stems or rhizomes up to 10 feet long that quickly invade the surrounding area. These ferns are not recommended for pot culture because of their coarseness and spreading rhizomes.

The 1½- to 2-foot-long fronds of the narrow-leaved chain ferns are divided into broad, pointed leaflets with wavy edges. Young sterile leaves are red, turning glossy green when mature. The spore-bearing fertile fronds that appear in late summer to fall are longer than sterile ones but have smooth-edged, extremely narrow leaflets. The giant chain fern grows 2 to 9 feet tall with broad, deeply lobed leaflets that look like enormous combs. The Virginia chain fern has fronds 2 to 4 feet long with 3-inch coarsely lobed leaflets. Fronds turn from yellow-green to deep green as they mature.

HOW TO GROW. Chain ferns grow outdoors in Zones 7-10. They do best in swampy areas where it is constantly wet. Plant the narrow-leaved chain fern in light to deep shade; the giant fern and Virginia chain fern thrive in open shade to full sun. In preparing new beds, use a mixture of 1 part garden loam, 1 part builder's sand and 2 parts leaf mold or peat moss. A pH of 5.5 to 6.5 is ideal. Propagate by dividing the underground stems in spring or from spores.

WOOLLY LIP FERN See *Cheilanthes*
WOOLLY TREE FERN See *Dicksonia*

For climate zones and frost dates, see maps, pages 146-147.

VIRGINIA CHAIN FERN
Woodwardia virginica

Appendix

Climate zones and frost dates

Although many of the ferns popular as house plants can be grown outdoors only in frost-free areas, a large number of attractive species are suitable for gardens as far north as Zone 3, as indicated in the encyclopedia entries, which are keyed to the map below. Some of these frost-resistant ferns, in fact, grow better in the North than in the South because they need a period of cold during their winter dormancy. Their fronds turn brown in fall in Zones 3, 4 and 5 but will remain nearly evergreen in Zone 6 and almost fully evergreen in Zones 7 and 8; although the plants are technically deciduous, the older fronds do not fall off until new spring growth emerges.

In choosing fern species for outdoor use, re-member that the zone map is, at best, a guide. Ferns sometimes grow outside of their preferred temperature range, but they may not grow as large, spread as quickly or live as long. And within any zone there are climate variations from mountain elevation to valley floor and from deep woods to sunny beaches.

Gardeners in cooler zones need not forsake the numerous attractive tropical ferns. They can be grown in pots indoors through the winter, then moved to the porch or patio for the summer. The maps at right, which indicate the dates of the last spring frost and the first fall frost for each area, show when it usually is safe to move the plants outside and when they should come back in.

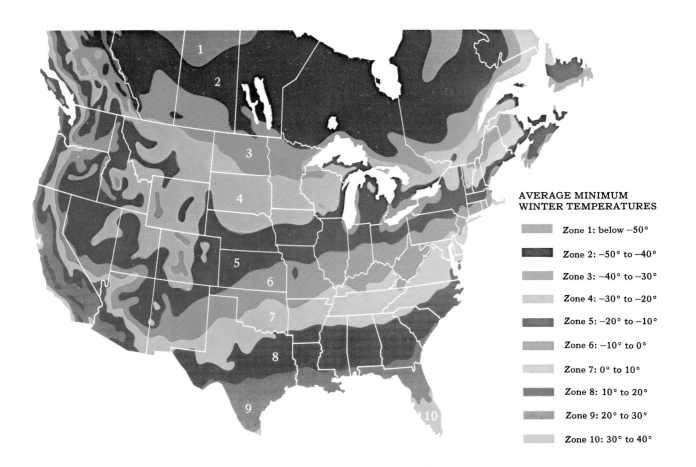

AVERAGE MINIMUM WINTER TEMPERATURES

Zone 1: below −50°

Zone 2: −50° to −40°

Zone 3: −40° to −30°

Zone 4: −30° to −20°

Zone 5: −20° to −10°

Zone 6: −10° to 0°

Zone 7: 0° to 10°

Zone 8: 10° to 20°

Zone 9: 20° to 30°

Zone 10: 30° to 40°

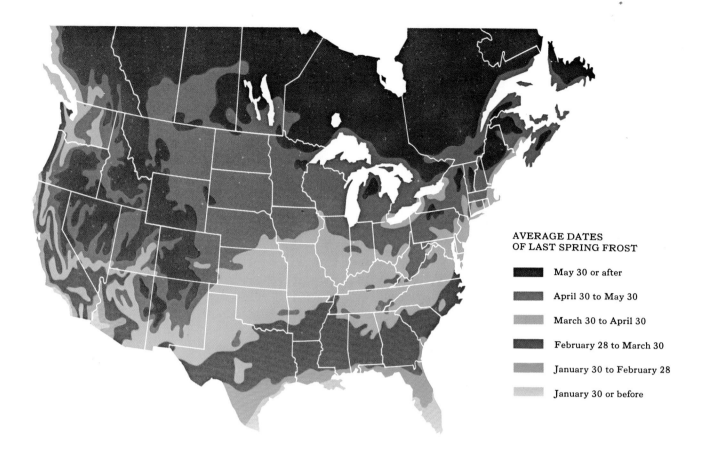

AVERAGE DATES
OF LAST SPRING FROST

█ May 30 or after

█ April 30 to May 30

█ March 30 to April 30

█ February 28 to March 30

█ January 30 to February 28

█ January 30 or before

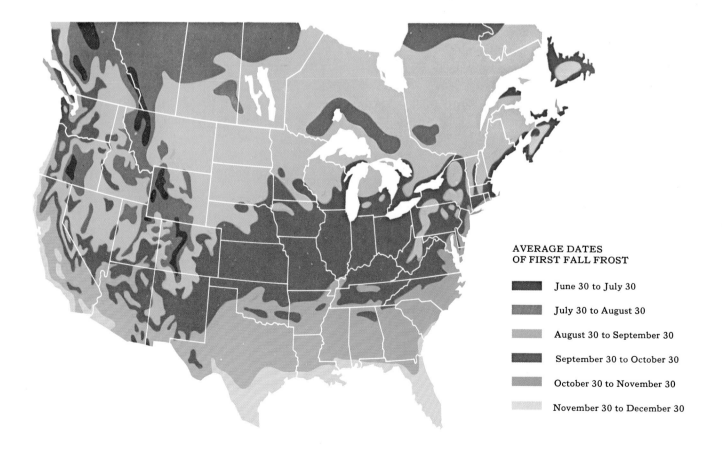

AVERAGE DATES
OF FIRST FALL FROST

█ June 30 to July 30

█ July 30 to August 30

█ August 30 to September 30

█ September 30 to October 30

█ October 30 to November 30

█ November 30 to December 30

147

Characteristics of 177 ferns

Fern	PLANT HEIGHT*				SOIL REQUIREMENTS						LIGHT NEEDS			SPECIAL USES								NIGHT TEMP.		
	Under 1 foot	1 to 3 feet	3 to 5 feet	Over 5 feet	Acid	Neutral	Alkaline	Dry	Moist	Wet	Open shade/800 ft. candles	Light shade/400 ft. candles	Deep shade/150 ft. candles	Ground cover	Bed and border	Accent plant	Rock garden	Potted plant	Dish garden or terrarium	Hanging basket	Water-filled container	45° to 55°	50° to 60°	60° to 70°
ACROSTICHUM AUREUM (leather fern)			●	●	●				●	●	●				●	●		●		●				●
ACROSTICHUM DANEAEFOLIUM (giant fern)			●	●					●	●	●				●	●		●		●				●
ACTINIOPTERIS AUSTRALIS	●					●	●		●		●				●	●	●	●						●
ADIANTUM CAPILLUS-VENERIS (southern maidenhair)	●	●				●			●		●				●	●	●	●					●	
ADIANTUM HISPIDULUM (rosy maidenhair)	●	●			●			●	●		●				●	●	●	●					●	
ADIANTUM MACROPHYLLUM	●				●				●		●				●	●	●	●					●	
ADIANTUM PEDATUM (northern maidenhair)	●	●			●				●		●				●	●	●	●					●	
ADIANTUM PERUVIANUM (silver-dollar fern)	●	●			●				●		●				●	●		●					●	
ADIANTUM RADDIANUM (delta maidenhair)	●	●			●				●		●				●	●	●	●					●	
ADIANTUM RADDIANUM 'PACIFIC MAID'	●				●				●		●				●	●	●	●					●	
ADIANTUM RADDIANUM VARIEGATUM	●	●			●				●		●				●	●	●	●					●	
ADIANTUM TENERUM (delicate maidenhair)		●					●		●		●				●	●	●	●					●	
ADIANTUM TENERUM WRIGHTII (fan maidenhair)		●					●		●		●				●	●	●	●					●	
ADIANTUM TRAPEZIFORME (diamond maidenhair)		●			●	●	●		●		●				●	●	●	●					●	
ALSOPHILA COOPERI (Australian tree fern)			●			●			●	●	●	●				●							●	
ANEMIA ADIANTIFOLIA (pine fern)	●	●			●			●	●		●	●			●		●							●
ANEMIA PHYLLITIDIS (flowering fern)	●	●			●			●	●		●	●			●		●							●
ANOGRAMMA CHAEROPHYLLA	●				●				●			●							●				●	
ASPLENIUM BULBIFERUM (mother fern)		●				●			●				●		●			●					●	
ASPLENIUM NIDUS (bird's-nest fern)		●	●			●			●				●		●	●		●					●	
ASPLENIUM NIDUS CRISPAFOLIUM		●				●			●				●		●	●		●					●	
ASPLENIUM PLATYNEURON (ebony spleenwort)	●	●				●			●		●	●			●	●	●					●		
ASPLENIUM TRICHOMANES (maidenhair spleenwort)	●					●			●		●	●			●	●	●					●		
ASPLENIUM VIVIPARUM (Mauritius mother fern)	●	●				●			●				●		●			●		●		●		
ATHYRIUM FILIX-FEMINA (lady fern)		●			●			●	●	●	●				●								●	
ATHYRIUM GOERINGIANUM PICTUM (Japanese painted fern)	●	●			●			●	●	●	●				●								●	
ATHYRIUM PYCNOCARPON (glade fern)			●			●		●	●	●	●				●								●	
ATHYRIUM THELYPTERIOIDES (silvery glade fern)		●			●			●	●	●	●				●								●	
AZOLLA CAROLINIANA (mosquito fern)	●				●				●	●								●			●	●		
AZOLLA FILICULOIDES (mosquito fern)	●				●				●	●								●			●	●		
BLECHNUM BRASILIENSE			●		●				●		●	●			●			●					●	
BLECHNUM GIBBUM			●		●				●		●	●			●			●					●	
BLECHNUM OCCIDENTALE (hammock fern)		●			●				●		●	●			●			●					●	
BLECHNUM SPICANT (deer fern)	●	●			●				●				●		●			●					●	
BOTRYCHIUM DISSECTUM (cut-leaved grape fern)	●	●				●			●			●		●								●		
BOTRYCHIUM MATRICARIAEFOLIUM (daisy-leaf grape fern)	●					●			●			●		●								●		
BOTRYCHIUM MULTIFIDA (leather grape fern)	●	●			●				●			●		●								●		
BOTRYCHIUM VIRGINIANUM (rattlesnake fern)	●	●			●				●			●		●								●		
CAMPTOSORUS RHIZOPHYLLUS (walking fern)	●						●		●		●						●		●				●	●
CERATOPTERIS PTERIDOIDES (American water fern)	●				●					●	●							●			●			●
CERATOPTERIS THALICTROIDES (Oriental water fern)	●				●					●	●							●			●			●
CETERACH AUREUM (rusty-back fern)	●	●			●			●	●		●				●			●				●		
CETERACH DALHOUSIAE	●				●			●	●		●				●			●				●		
CETERACH OFFICINARUM (scale fern)	●					●	●	●	●		●				●			●				●		
CHEILANTHES GRACILLIMA (lace fern)	●				●			●	●		●				●		●	●				●		
CHEILANTHES LANOSA (hairy lip fern)	●				●			●	●				●		●		●	●				●		
CHEILANTHES TOMENTOSA (woolly lip fern)	●				●			●	●		●				●		●	●				●		
CIBOTIUM BAROMETZ (Scythian lamb)			●			●			●		●					●		●					●	
CIBOTIUM GLAUCUM (Hawaiian tree fern)			●	●					●		●					●		●					●	

In the case of arching ferns, figures apply to length of fronds.

	PLANT HEIGHT*				SOIL REQUIREMENTS						LIGHT NEEDS			SPECIAL USES								NIGHT TEMP.		
	Under 1 foot	1 to 3 feet	3 to 5 feet	Over 5 feet	Acid	Neutral	Alkaline	Dry	Moist	Wet	Open shade/800 ft. candles	Light shade/400 ft. candles	Deep shade/150 ft. candles	Ground cover	Bed and border	Accent plant	Rock garden	Potted plant	Dish garden or terrarium	Hanging basket	Water-filled container	45° to 55°	50° to 60°	60° to 70°
CIBOTIUM SCHIEDEI (Mexican tree fern)		●	●		●				●				●		●		●						●	
CRYPTOGRAMMA CRISPA (American rock brake)	●			●	●				●				●			●					●		●	
CYATHEA ARBOREA (West Indian tree fern)			●		●				●				●		●		●							●
CYATHEA DEALBATA (silver tree fern)			●		●				●				●		●		●						●	
CYATHEA MEDULLARIS (black tree fern)			●		●			●	●	●			●		●		●						●	
CYCLOPHORUS LINGUA (Japanese felt fern)	●				●				●			●	●		●		●		●					●
CYRTOMIUM FALCATUM (holly fern)	●	●			●			●	●				●		●	●	●						●	
CYRTOMIUM FALCATUM CARYOTIDEUM	●	●				●	●	●					●		●	●	●						●	
CYRTOMIUM FALCATUM ROCHEFORDIANUM (Rocheford's holly fern)	●	●			●			●	●				●		●	●	●						●	
CYRTOMIUM FORTUNEI	●	●			●			●	●				●		●	●	●						●	
CYSTOPTERIS BULBIFERA (bulblet bladder fern)	●	●				●			●			●				●					●		●	
CYSTOPTERIS FRAGILIS (fragile bladder fern)	●					●			●			●				●					●		●	
DAVALLIA FEJEENSIS (Fiji davallia)		●			●				●	●	●	●		●		●		●			●			●
DAVALLIA MARIESII (ball fern)	●				●				●	●	●	●		●		●		●			●		●	
DAVALLIA SOLIDA (Polynesian davallia)		●			●				●	●	●	●		●		●		●			●			●
DENNSTAEDTIA CICUTARIA (common cup fern)		●	●	●				●			●	●											●	
DENNSTAEDTIA PUNCTILOBULA (hay-scented fern)		●			●				●			●	●									●		
DICKSONIA ANTARCTICA (Tasmanian dicksonia)		●	●	●		●			●	●			●		●								●	
DICKSONIA FIBROSA (woolly tree fern)		●	●	●		●			●	●			●		●								●	
DICKSONIA SQUARROSA (slender tree fern)		●	●	●		●			●	●			●		●								●	
DIPLAZIUM ESCULENTUM (vegetable fern)		●			●				●	●	●				●								●	
DIPLAZIUM PROLIFERUM		●			●				●	●	●				●								●	
DOODIA MAXIMA (hacksaw fern)		●		●		●	●		●								●	●	●	●			●	
DOODIA MEDIA (hacksaw fern)		●		●		●	●		●								●	●	●	●			●	
DORYOPTERIS CONCOLOR		●		●					●			●			●		●							●
DORYOPTERIS PEDATA PALMATA (spear-leaved fern)		●		●					●			●			●		●							●
DRYNARIA QUERCIFOLIA (oak-leaf fern)		●		●		●	●	●							●					●				●
DRYNARIA RIGIDULA		●		●		●	●	●							●					●				●
DRYOPTERIS AMPLA (American tree fern)		●				●			●						●								●	
DRYOPTERIS ARGUTA (coastal wood fern)		●			●				●		●	●			●								●	
DRYOPTERIS CRISTATA (crested shield fern)		●			●				●	●	●				●								●	
DRYOPTERIS DECOMPOSITA		●			●			●										●					●	
DRYOPTERIS FILIX-MAS (male fern)		●	●		●				●			●			●								●	
DRYOPTERIS FILIX-MAS CRISTATA (crested male fern)		●	●		●				●			●			●								●	
DRYOPTERIS GOLDIANA (Goldie's fern)			●		●				●	●					●								●	
DRYOPTERIS LINNAEANA (oak fern)	●				●				●			●		●		●							●	
DRYOPTERIS NOVEBORACENSIS (New York fern)		●			●				●	●					●								●	
DRYOPTERIS SPINULOSA INTERMEDIA (buckler fern)		●			●				●		●				●								●	
EQUISETUM HYEMALE (scouring rush)			●		●			●	●	●			●								●		●	
EQUISETUM SCORPIODES (dwarf scouring rush)	●				●			●	●	●			●								●		●	
EQUISETUM VARIEGATUM (variegated scouring rush)		●			●			●	●	●			●					●			●		●	
HEMIONITIS ARIFOLIA	●	●			●				●		●							●	●					●
HEMIONITIS PALMATA (strawberry fern)	●				●				●		●							●	●					●
HUMATA TYERMANNII (bear's-foot fern)	●					●	●		●	●		●	●		●	●	●	●	●	●			●	
HYMENOPHYLLUM DEMISSUM (filmy fern)	●				●				●	●			●							●			●	
HYPOLEPIS PUNCTATA		●	●		●				●			●	●	●	●			●					●	
HYPOLEPIS REPENS (bramble fern)		●	●		●				●			●	●	●	●			●					●	
LEMMAPHYLLUM MICROPHYLLUM	●				●				●									●	●					●
LYGODIUM JAPONICUM (Japanese climbing fern)		●	●	●		●			●	●		●						●		●			●	

CHARACTERISTICS OF FERNS: CONTINUED

	PLANT HEIGHT*				SOIL REQUIREMENTS						LIGHT NEEDS			SPECIAL USES								NIGHT TEMP.		
	Under 1 foot	1 to 3 feet	3 to 5 feet	Over 5 feet	Acid	Neutral	Alkaline	Dry	Moist	Wet	Open shade/800 ft. candles	Light shade/400 ft. candles	Deep shade/150 ft. candles	Ground cover	Bed and border	Accent plant	Rock garden	Potted plant	Dish garden or terrarium	Hanging basket	Water-filled container	45° to 55°	50° to 60°	60° to 70°
LYGODIUM PALMATUM (Hartford fern)			●	●	●				●		●	●	●										●	
MARSILEA QUADRIFOLIA (water clover fern)	●				●				●	●									●		●	●	●	
MATTEUCCIA STRUTHIOPTERIS (ostrich fern)			●	●	●				●	●	●	●					●						●	
MICROLEPIA PLATYPHYLLA			●	●				●	●			●				●							●	
MICROLEPIA SPELUNCAE			●	●	●			●	●			●				●							●	
MICROLEPIA STRIGOSA		●	●		●			●	●	●						●		●					●	
NEPHROLEPIS BISERRATA FURCANS (fishtail sword fern)		●			●			●	●	●	●	●	●		●	●	●		●				●	
NEPHROLEPIS CORDIFOLIA DUFFII (Duff's sword fern)		●			●			●	●		●	●	●		●	●	●		●				●	
NEPHROLEPIS EXALTATA BOSTONIENSIS (Boston fern)		●			●			●	●		●	●	●		●	●	●		●				●	
NEPHROLEPIS EXALTATA BOSTONIENSIS COMPACTA (dwarf Boston fern)	●	●			●			●	●		●	●	●		●	●	●		●				●	
NEPHROLEPIS EXALTATA 'FLUFFY RUFFLES'		●			●			●	●		●	●	●		●	●	●		●				●	
NEPHROLEPIS EXALTATA 'MINI-RUFFLE'	●				●			●	●		●	●	●		●	●	●		●				●	
NEPHROLEPIS EXALTATA NORWOODII (Norwood sword fern)		●			●			●	●		●	●	●		●	●	●		●				●	
ONOCLEA SENSIBILIS (sensitive fern)		●			●				●	●				●	●							●		
ONYCHIUM JAPONICUM (Japanese claw fern)	●				●				●			●		●	●								●	
OPHIOGLOSSUM PETIOIATUM (southern adder's-tongue)	●				●				●	●								●	●	●			●	
OPHIOGLOSSUM VULGATUM (northern adder's-tongue)	●				●				●	●								●					●	
OSMUNDA CINNAMOMEA (cinnamon fern)		●	●		●				●	●		●			●	●						●	●	●
OSMUNDA CLAYTONIA (interrupted fern)		●			●	●			●			●			●	●						●	●	●
OSMUNDA REGALIS (royal fern)			●	●	●				●	●		●			●	●						●	●	●
PELLAEA ATROPURPUREA (purple cliff brake)		●				●	●	●			●				●		●	●		●			●	
PELLAEA BRACHYPTERA (Sierra cliff brake)		●					●	●			●				●		●	●		●			●	
PELLAEA DENSA (Indian's dream)	●				●			●	●		●				●		●	●		●			●	
PELLAEA FALCATA (Australian cliff brake)	●	●			●			●	●	●					●		●	●		●			●	
PELLAEA ROTUNDIFOLIA (button fern)	●				●			●	●	●					●		●	●		●			●	
PELLAEA VIRIDIS VIRIDIS (green cliff brake)		●			●			●	●	●					●		●	●		●			●	
PHYLLITIS SCOLOPENDRIUM (hart's-tongue fern)		●				●			●			●			●		●	●					●	
PITYROGRAMMA ARGENTEA (goldback fern)		●			●				●			●				●		●		●				●
PITYROGRAMMA CALOMELANOS (silver fern)		●			●				●			●				●		●		●				●
PITYROGRAMMA CHRYSOPHYLLA (gold fern)		●			●				●			●				●		●		●				●
PITYROGRAMMA TRIANGULARIS (California goldback fern)		●			●			●	●			●				●		●	●	●		●		
PLATYCERIUM ANGOLENSE (Angola staghorn fern)			●		●				●		●	●				●				●				●
PLATYCERIUM BIFURCATUM (staghorn fern)		●	●		●				●		●	●				●				●			●	●
PLATYCERIUM BIFURCATUM 'SAN DIEGO' (San Diego staghorn)		●	●		●				●		●	●				●				●				●
PLATYCERIUM GRANDE		●	●		●				●		●	●				●				●			●	●
PLATYCERIUM HILLII		●	●		●				●		●	●				●				●			●	●
PLATYCERIUM VASSEI		●			●				●		●	●				●				●				●
PLATYCERIUM WILLINCKII (Java staghorn fern)		●			●				●		●	●				●				●				●
POLYPODIUM ANGUSTIFOLIUM (narrow-leaved strap fern)		●			●				●			●				●		●	●	●			●	
POLYPODIUM AUREUM (rabbit's-foot fern)		●			●				●	●						●		●	●	●			●	
POLYPODIUM CORONANS		●			●				●	●						●		●	●	●			●	
POLYPODIUM CRASSIFOLIUM		●			●				●		●					●		●	●	●			●	
POLYPODIUM GLYCYRRHIZA (licorice fern)		●			●				●		●					●		●	●	●		●		
POLYPODIUM LYCOPODIOIDES	●				●				●		●					●		●	●	●			●	
POLYPODIUM POLYCARPON GRANDICEPS (climbing bird's-nest)		●			●				●		●					●		●	●	●			●	
POLYPODIUM POLYPODIOIDES (resurrection fern)	●				●				●		●					●		●	●	●			●	
POLYPODIUM SCOULERI (leathery polypody)		●			●				●		●					●		●	●	●			●	
POLYPODIUM SUBAURICULATUM (jointed polypody)			●	●	●				●			●				●		●	●	●			●	
POLYPODIUM VULGARE (common polypody)	●				●				●			●				●		●	●	●		●		

In the case of arching ferns, figures apply to length of fronds.

	PLANT HEIGHT*				SOIL REQUIREMENTS						LIGHT NEEDS			SPECIAL USES								NIGHT TEMP.		
	Under 1 foot	1 to 3 feet	3 to 5 feet	Over 5 feet	Acid	Neutral	Alkaline	Dry	Moist	Wet	Open shade/800 ft. candles	Light shade/400 ft. candles	Deep shade/150 ft. candles	Ground cover	Bed and border	Accent plant	Rock garden	Potted plant	Dish garden or terrarium	Hanging basket	Water-filled container	45° to 55°	50° to 60°	60° to 70°
POLYSTICHUM ACROSTICHOIDES (Christmas fern)		●			●			●			●		●	●	●		●		●		●			
POLYSTICHUM ADIANTIFORME (leather fern)		●			●			●				●		●	●		●		●			●		
POLYSTICHUM ARISTATUM (East Indian holly fern)		●			●			●				●		●	●		●		●		●			
POLYSTICHUM MUNITUM (western sword fern)		●			●			●					●	●	●		●		●		●			
POLYSTICHUM SETIFERUM (soft shield fern)		●			●				●			●		●	●		●		●			●		
POLYSTICHUM STANDISHII (upside-down fern)		●			●				●			●			●	●			●			●		
POLYSTICHUM TSUS-SIMENSE (Tsussima holly fern)	●				●				●			●					●	●		●			●	
PTERIDIUM AQUILINUM (bracken fern)		●			●	●		●			●													●
PTERIDIUM AQUILINUM LATIUSCULUM (eastern bracken fern)		●			●	●		●	●		●													●
PTERIS BIAURITA		●			●				●			●	●	●	●								●	
PTERIS BIAURITA ARGYRAEA (silver brake fern)		●			●				●			●	●	●	●								●	
PTERIS CRETICA (Cretan brake fern)	●				●				●			●		●	●								●	
PTERIS CRETICA ALBO-LINEATA (ribbon brake fern)	●				●				●			●		●	●								●	
PTERIS ENSIFORMIS (sword brake fern)	●	●			●				●			●		●	●								●	
PTERIS MULTIFIDA (spider brake fern)		●			●				●			●		●	●	●	●						●	
PTERIS TREMULA (trembling brake fern)			●		●				●			●		●	●	●							●	
SALVINIA NATANS	●				●					●	●									●	●			●
SALVINIA ROTUNDIFOLIA (water spangles)	●				●				●		●									●	●			●
SCYPHULARIA PENTAPHYLLA (monkey's-paw fern)	●					●	●		●				●			●			●					●
SELAGINELLA KRAUSSIANA (spreading selaginella)	●				●				●	●		●	●		●	●	●						●	
TECTARIA GEMMIFERA (button fern)		●			●				●			●			●	●	●						●	
TODEA BARBARA (crape fern)		●			●				●	●			●		●								●	
TRICHOMANES PETERSII	●								●				●					●					●	
TRICHOMANES RADICANS (bristle fern)	●								●				●					●					●	
WOODSIA ILVENSIS (rusty woodsia)	●				●			●	●		●			●			●				●			
WOODSIA OBTUSA (blunt-lobed woodsia)	●					●		●	●		●			●			●				●			
WOODSIA SCOPULINA (mountain woodsia)	●				●			●	●		●			●	●						●			
WOODWARDIA AREOLATA (narrow-leaved chain fern)		●			●				●	●	●			●	●								●	
WOODWARDIA FIMBRIATA (giant chain fern)		●	●	●	●				●	●				●	●								●	
WOODWARDIA VIRGINICA (Virginia chain fern)		●	●		●				●	●				●	●								●	

Picture credits

The sources for the illustrations in this book are shown below. Credits from left to right are separated by semicolons, from top to bottom by dashes. Cover—Peter B. Kaplan. 4—Philip Perl; Richard Crist. 6—G. Rodway from Alison Rutherford, courtesy Glasgow Museums. 8—Drawings by Sue Johnston. 11—Courtesy Smithsonian Institution. 13—A. Murray Evans. 14—Lynn Pelham; A. Murray Evans (3)—Sue Olsen; Maurice Broun; A. Murray Evans. 15—A. Murray Evans except top right B. J. Hoshizaki. 16—A. Murray Evans (2); B. J. Hoshizaki—A. Murray Evans (2); B. J. Hoshizaki—B. J. Hoshizaki (2). 19—Drawings by William Coulter. 20—William Hemmer. 21—Laurel Bird. 24—John A. Lynch. 29—Robert Dunne/National Audubon Society Collection/PR. 30, 31, 33—Drawings by Kathy Rebeiz. 36—Drawings by William Coulter. 39—Drawings by Kathy Rebeiz. 43—Sue Olsen, courtesy of Roy Davidson. 44, 45—Lynn Pelham. 46, 47—Entheos, courtesy of William Street. 48, 49—Bob Waterman. 50—Peter B. Kaplan. 55, 59, 61—Drawings by William Coulter. 65 through 73—Peter B. Kaplan. 74—Winton Patnode, 1965 National Audubon Society Collection/PR. 76, 77, 79—Drawings by William Coulter. 81—Ted Streshinsky, courtesy of John Ekstrand. 82, 83—Ted Streshinsky. 85, 87—Drawings by William Coulter. 88 through 145—Encyclopedia illustrations by Richard Crist. 146, 147—Maps by Adolph E. Brotman.

Acknowledgments

The index for this book was prepared by Anita R. Beckerman. For their help in the preparation of this book, the editors wish to thank the following: Virginia Ault, Miami Springs, Florida; Maurice Broun, New Ringgold, Pennsylvania; Jesse Brown, National Agricultural Library, Beltsville, Maryland; John Ekstrand, Fernut Nursery, Orange, California; Dr. A. Murray Evans, Department of Botany, University of Tennessee, Knoxville, Tennessee; Prof. Joseph Ewan, Tulane University, New Orleans, Louisiana; Derek Fell, Gardenville, Pennsylvania; Dr. Gerald Gastony, Department of Biology, Indiana University, Bloomington, Indiana; Elizabeth C. Hall, Senior Librarian, Horticultural Society of New York, New York City; Barbara Heinen, Horticultural Society of New York, New York City; William Hemmer, Miami, Florida; Dr. Francis M. Hueber, Curator, Division of Paleobotany, National Museum of Natural History, Smithsonian Institution, Washington, D.C.; Craig T. Keys, National Arboretum, Washington, D.C.; W. P. Lee, Lee Nursery, Panama City, Florida; Dr. David B. Lellinger, Curator of Ferns, National Museum of Natural History, Smithsonian Institution, Washington, D.C.; Dr. Robert Lloyd, Botany Department, Ohio University, Athens, Ohio; Barbara McMartin, Croton-on-Hudson, New York; Everitt Miller, Assistant Director, Longwood Gardens, Kennett Square, Pennsylvania; Mildred Murray, Encinitas, California; Bruce Nash, Alexandria Floral Co., Alexandria, Virginia; The National Herbarium, Smithsonian Institution, Washington, D.C.; Suzanne Olsen, Bellevue, Washington; Wilbur Olson, Redondo Beach, California; Mr. and Mrs. W. F. Radcliffe, Lake Placid, Florida; Rolfe W. Smith, Section Head, Ferns and Tropical Terrace Garden, Longwood Gardens, Kennett Square, Pennsylvania; South Florida Fern Society, Inc., Miami, Florida; William G. Teufel and Associates, Inc., Seattle, Washington; Steven C. Wilson, Bainbridge Island, Washington.

Bibliography

Abrams, LeRoy, *Illustrated Flora of the Pacific States* (4 vols.). Stanford University Press, 1960.

Allan, Mea, *Tradescants: Their Plants, Gardens, and Museum 1570-1622.* Michael Joseph, 1964.

Allen, David Elliston, *The Victorian Fern Craze: A History of Pteridomania.* Hutchinson of London, 1969.

Andrews, Henry N., Jr., *Ancient Plants and the World They Lived In.* Cornell University Press, 1947.

Andrews, Michael and Hunt, Peter, *The Marshall Cavenish Encyclopedia of Gardening.* Marshall Cavenish, Ltd., 1968.

Ashberry, Anne, *Bottle Gardens and Fern Cases.* Hodder & Stoughton, 1964.

Atkinson, Robert E., *The Complete Book of Groundcovers.* David McKay, 1970.

Bailey, L. H., *Manual of Cultivated Plants.* Macmillan Publishing Co., Inc., 1938.

Bailey, L. H., *The Standard Cyclopedia of Horticulture* (3 vols.). Macmillan Publishing Co., Inc., 1900.

Bastin, Harold, *Plants without Flowers.* Philosophical Library, 1955.

Benedict, R. C., "The Most Fundamental Discovery About Ferns," *American Fern Journal,* Vol. 45, April-June, 1955.

Birdseye, Clarence and Eleanor G., *Growing Woodland Plants.* Dover Publications, Inc., 1972.

Birkenhead, John, *Ferns and Fern Culture.* Privately published, 1897.

Blake, Claire L., *Greenhouse Gardening for Fun.* William Morrow and Co., Inc., 1972.

Blomquist, Hugo L., *Ferns of North Carolina.* Cambridge University Press, 1935.

Brooklyn Botanic Garden, *Handbook on Ferns.* BBG, 1975.

Broun, Maurice, *Index to the North American Ferns.* Privately published, 1938.

Chabot, Ernest, *The New Greenhouse Gardening for Everyone.* M. Barrows and Co., Inc., 1955.

Chittenden, Fred J., ed., *The Royal Horticultural Society Dictionary of Gardening,* 2nd ed. Clarendon Press, 1974.

Clute, Willard Nelson, *Our Ferns; Their Haunts, Habits and Folklore.* Frederick A. Stokes Company, 1938.

Cobb, Boughton, *A Field Guide to the Ferns.* Houghton Mifflin Company, 1956.

Copeland, Edwin Bingham, "Edible Ferns," *American Fern Journal,* Vol. 32, No. 4, Oct.-Dec., 1942.

Copeland, Edwin Bingham, *Genera Filicium, The Genera of Ferns.* Chronica Botanica Co., 1974.

Crabbe, J. A., Jermy, A. C., and Mickel, J. T., "A New Generic Sequence for the Pteridophyte Herbarium," *Fern Gazette,* Vol. II, part 2 & 3, 1975.

Crockett, James Underwood, *Foliage Plants for Indoor Gardening.* Doubleday & Co., Inc., 1967.

Druery, Charles Thomas, *British Ferns and Their Varieties.* G. Routledge and Sons, 1912.

Druery, Charles Thomas, *Choice British Ferns.* L. U. Gill, 1888.

Durand, Herbert, *Field Book of Common Ferns.* Putnam, 1949.

Eaton, Daniel Cady, *The Ferns of North America.* S. E. Cassimo, 1879-1880.

Ellison, Patricia, Kingsbury, John M., and Hyypio, Peter A., *Common Wild Flowers of New York State,* Cornell Extension Bulletin 990, 1973.

Evans, Charles M. and Pliner, Roberta Lee, *The Terrarium Book.* Random House, 1973.

Everett, T. H., ed., *New Illustrated Encyclopedia of Gardening.* Greystone Press, 1967.

Ewan, Joseph, "First Fern Records from Virginia: John Banister's Account of 1679-1692," *American Fern Journal,* Vol. 53, No. 4, Oct.-Dec., 1963.

Foster, F. Gordon, *Ferns to Know and Grow.* Hawthorn Books, 1971.

Foster, F. Gordon, *The Gardeners Fern Book.* Van Nostrand, 1964.

Franks, Wendy, *Platycerium—Fern Facts.* Privately published, 1969.

Frye, Theodore C., *Ferns of the Northwest.* Metropolitan Press, 1934.

Galle, Fred C., *Azaleas.* Oxmoor House, 1974.

Gleason, Henry A., *The New Britton and Brown Illustrated Flora of the Northeastern United States and Adjacent Canada* (3 vols.). The New York Botanical Garden, 1952.

Graf, Alfred Byrd, *Exotic Plant Manual,* 4th ed. Roehrs Co., Inc., 1974.

Graf, Alfred Byrd, *Exotica,* Series 3, 8th ed. Roehrs Co., Inc., 1976.

Grillos, Steve J., *Ferns and Fern Allies of California.* University of California Press, 1966.

Hancock, F. D. and Lucas, A., *Ferns of the Witwatersrand.* Witwatersrand University Press, Johannesburg, 1973.

Hanging Plants for Modern Living. Merchants Publishing Co., 1975.

Hemsley, Alfred, *The Book of Fern Culture.* J. Lane Co., 1908.

Hibberd, Shirley, *The Fern Garden.* Groombridge and Sons, 1869.

Hibberd, Shirley, *Rustic Adornments for Homes of Taste.* W. H. & L. Collingridge, 1895.

Hodge, W. H., "Fern Foods of Japan and the Problem of Toxicity," *American Fern Journal,* Vol. 63, No. 3, 1973.

Holttum, Richard Eric, *A Revised Flora of Malaya, 2,* "Ferns," 2nd ed. Government Printing Office, Singapore, 1968.

Hooker, William J., *Species Filicum* (2 vols.). Verlag Von J.

Cramer, reprinted 1970.

Hoshizaki, Barbara Joe, *Fern Growers Manual.* Alfred A. Knopf, 1975.

Hoshizaki, Barbara Joe, "The Genus *Adiantum* in Cultivation (*Polypodiacea*)," *Baileya,* Vol. 17, Autumn, 1970.

Hylander, Clarence J., *The World of Plant Life,* 2nd ed. Macmillan, 1956.

Joe, Barbara, "The Bracken Fern," *Lasca Leaves,* Autumn, 1963.

Joe, Barbara, "Cup Ferns *(Dennstaedtia)* Cultivated in California," *American Fern Journal,* Vol. 55, No. 2, 1965.

Joe, Barbara, "Ferns Cultivated in California: *Hypolepis,*" *Lasca Leaves,* Vol. 9, Autumn, 1959.

Kepler, Kay, *Common Ferns of Loquillo Forest,* Inter-American University Press, 1975.

Kingsbury, John M., *Common Poisonous Plants.* Cornell Extension Bulletin 538, 1972.

Knobloch, Irving W. and Lellinger, David B., "*Cheilanthes castanea* and its Allies in Virginia and West Virginia," *Castanea,* Vol. 34, 1969.

Kramer, Jack, *Ferns and Palms for Interior Decoration.* Charles Scribner's Sons, 1972.

Kranz, Frederick H. and Jacqueline L., *Gardening Indoors Under Lights.* Viking, 1971.

Langer, Richard W., *Grow it Indoors.* Saturday Review Press, 1975.

Lellinger, David, "The Correct Name for the Button Fern," *American Fern Journal,* Vol. 58, No. 4, 1968.

Lichten, Frances, *Decorative Art of Victoria's Era.* Charles Scribner's Sons, 1950.

Lowe, E. J., *Ferns: British and Exotic* (8 vols.). Groombridge and Sons, 1856-1860.

McVaugh, Rogers and Pyron, Joseph H., *Ferns of Georgia.* University of Georgia Press, 1951.

Macself, Albert James, *Ferns for Garden and Greenhouse.* Transatlantic Arts, Inc., 1952.

Massey, Arthur Ballard, *The Ferns and Fern Allies of Virginia.* Virginia Polytechnic Institute, 1944.

Mazzeo, Peter M., "Ferns and Fern Allies of Shenandoah National Park." Shenandoah National History Association, Bulletin #6, 1972.

Miles, Bebe, *Bluebells and Bittersweet.* Van Nostrand Reinhold, 1970.

Mohlenbrock, R. H., *The Illustrated Flora of Illinois—Ferns.* Southern Illinois University Press, 1967.

Morse, Harriet K., *Gardening in the Shade.* Charles Scribner's Sons, 1962.

Morton, C. V., "Observations on Cultivated Ferns IV, The Species of *Davallia,*" *American Fern Journal,* Vol. 47, No. 4, 1957.

Morton, C. V., "Observations on Cultivated Ferns V, The Species and Forms of *Nephrolepis,*" *American Fern Journal,* Vol. 48, No. 1, 1958.

Native Ferns of Eastern North America. Toronto, Canada Audubon Society, 1963.

Parsons, Frances Theodora, *How to Know the Ferns,* 4th ed. Charles Scribner's Sons, 1907.

Perry, Frances, ed., *Simon and Schuster's Complete Guide to Plants and Flowers.* 1976.

Reader's Digest, *Complete Book of the Garden.* Reader's Digest Association, 1966.

Reed, Clyde F., *The Ferns and Fern Allies of Maryland and Delaware.* Reed Herbarium, 1953.

Roberts, Edith A. and Lawrence, Julia R., *American Ferns.* Macmillan Publishing Co., Inc., 1935.

Robinson, John, *Ferns in Their Homes and Ours.* S. E. Cassimo, 1878.

Rovirosa, José, N., *Pteridografica del sur de Mexico.* Impr. de Escalante, 1909.

Sanders, T. W., *Encyclopedia of Gardening,* 22nd ed., revised by A. G. L. Hellyer in *The Gardener's Golden Treasury.* Transatlantic Arts, Inc., 1956.

Schneider, George, *Choice Ferns for Amateurs* (3 vols.). Charles Scribner's Sons, 1905.

Seymour, E. L. D., ed., *The Wise Garden Encyclopedia.* Grosset & Dunlap, 1970.

Shaver, Jesse M., *Ferns of Tennessee.* Peabody College, 1954.

Singleton, Esther, *The Shakespeare Garden.* William Farquhar Payson, 1931.

Small, John Kunkel, *Ferns of the Southeastern States.* Science Press, 1938.

Staff of the L. H. Bailey Hortorium, Cornell University, *Hortus Third: A Dictionary of Plants Cultivated in the United States and Canada.* Macmillan Publishing Co., Inc., 1976.

Stark, Francis B. and Link, Conrad B., *Rock Gardens and Water Plants in Color.* Doubleday, 1969.

Stodola, Jiri, *Encyclopedia of Water Plants.* T. F. H. Publications, 1967.

Stokoe, W. J., *The Observer's Book of Ferns.* revised ed. Frederick Warne, 1965.

Sunset Books, *Ideas for Hanging Gardens.* Lane Publishing Co., 1974.

Sunset Books, *Western Garden Book.* Lane Publishing Co., 1954.

Svenson, H. K., "The New World Species of *Azolla,*" *American Fern Journal,* Vol. 34, July-Sept., 1944.

Swindells, Philip, *Ferns for Garden and Greenhouse.* International Publications Service, 1971.

Taylor, Norman, ed., *Taylor's Encyclopedia of Gardening,* 4th ed. Houghton Mifflin, 1961.

Taylor, Thomas C., *Pacific Northwest Ferns and Their Allies.* University of Toronto Press, 1970.

Tergit, Gabriele, *Flowers through the Ages.* Oswald Wolff, 1961.

Tryon, Rolla and Alice, "Observations on Cultivated Tree Ferns *(Dicksonia* and *Cyathea)*," *American Fern Journal,* Vol. 49, No. 4, 1959.

United States Department of Agriculture, *Trees, The Yearbook of Agriculture 1949.* United States Government Printing Office, 1949.

Von Miklos, Josephine and Fiore, E. L., *The Gardener's World.* Ridge Press, 1969.

Wakefield, N. A., *The Ferns of Victoria and Tasmania.* Field Naturalists' Club of Victoria, 1955.

Wherry, Edgar T., *The Fern Guide.* Doubleday, 1961.

Wherry, Edgar T., *The Southern Fern Guide.* Doubleday, 1964.

Wiley, Farida A., *Ferns of Northeastern United States.* Peter Smith Publisher, Inc., 1973.

Wilson, C. L., Loomis, W. E., and Steeres, T. A., *Botany,* 5th ed. Holt, Rhinehart and Winston, 1971.

Wilson, Lois, *The Complete Gardener.* Hawthorn Books, 1972.

Witham, H., *Ferns of San Diego County.* San Diego Natural History Museum, 1972.

Woolson, Grace A., *Ferns and How to Grow Them.* Doubleday Page & Co., 1914.

Wyman, Donald, *Wyman's Gardening Encyclopedia.* Macmillan Publishing Co., Inc., 1971.

Youngman, Wilbur H., "Garden Book," *Washington Star-News,* 1962-1976.

Index